Beadweaving
Beyond the Basics

24 beading designs using
seed beads, crystals,
two-hole beads and more

Kassie Shaw

Fons&Porter

Cincinnati, Ohio

Dedication

To my parents, Rex and Doris, who taught me to shoot for the stars. Because of you, I know that I can accomplish anything.

To my children, Johnathan and Faith, who put up with a year's worth of me as an overextended mom but encouraged me all the same. Especially for Faith, who was the best model I could have hoped for and without whom this book would be less beautiful.

Acknowledgments

Thank you to my wonderful pattern testers and sample makers! Especially Annette Holbert and Sherry Mamet, who between the two of them made just about every project in the book. My thanks also go out to D. Aryd'ell Hotelling, Mary Jo Leonard, Susan Council, Linda Roberts, Valorie Clifton, Pat Keran, Bev Moon, Pam Hauser and Nancy Dale.

Thank you to Amelia Johanson, my acquisitions editor, who helped me to put together a great proposal, to Noel Rivera and Christine Doyle, my content and layout editors, who kept me on task and made sure that my intent was reflected in my words, to Ronson Slagle, my designer, for making my book beautiful, and to Kendra Lapolla, my illustrator, who made my diagrams come to life.

Thank you to my terrific crew on four amazing photo shoots:

Hannah Combs, whose beautiful photos bring out the best in my work.

My models: Faith Inman, Kimberly Serena, Sarah Montgomery, Ariel Manis and Patrice Wilson.

Hair by Tyler Creek, Joanne Bolet Cafaro and Amy Day Daugherty.

Makeup by Kimberly Serena and Sarah Montgomery.

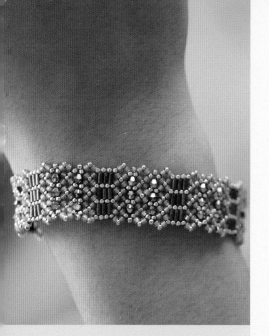

Contents

Introduction

As a designer and an artist, I'm passionate about discovering new, innovative ideas and sharing those ideas with others. I often get barely halfway through a project when I discover new directions I could take to create something completely different. Even my mistakes can be inspirational; for instance, sometimes I cut something apart and see a shape I like or a thread path I hadn't considered before. My goal in writing this book is not only to teach you, my reader, how to create the pieces I've designed but also to inspire you to discover your own creativity and ideas.

HOW TO USE THIS BOOK

The most important rule to remember in beading is that there are no rules! The main purpose of this book is to teach you some intermediate variations on basic stitches and how to use them as jumping-off points for your own designs. If it suits you, you can read this book in order from front to back. This will give you insight into my own design methods, as the order of the projects is intended to show how I progressed from one project into the next.

Each chapter in this book is a study of variation. While the primary focus of the book is based on right angle weave (RAW), the three chapters will teach you multiple ways to use a few of my favorite RAW variations: double diamond right angle weave (DDRAW), faux right angle weave (FRAW)

and layered right angle weave (LRAW). I haven't, however, eschewed other stitches completely for RAW. In case you need a refresher, you'll find some of my other favorite stitches (such as herringbone, peyote and St. Petersburg) described in My Favorite Stitches on page 11.

All of the techniques and projects feature diagrams. The darker/brighter beads represent beads being added during that step. Lighter beads represent beads that have

been added in previous steps. The dot on each thread path will be shown on the bead the thread is exiting at the beginning of that step.

As you work your way through this book, please feel free to drop me a line. If you finish a piece, I would love to see a photograph and may even post it in a gallery of my

designs made by others. Even more important, though, is that I want to help if you get stuck. If you are having difficulty with a particular design of mine, or if you've had an idea of your own but wonder how best to approach it, e-mail me at kassie@beadingbutterfly .com so I can assist you.

My Favorite Materials & Tools

I've been making jewelry for almost ten years, and one thing I learned very quickly is that every beader has his or her own idea of what materials and tools are the best to use for the job. I won't be going into too much detail about all of the various options there are for beads, beading supplies and tools, but I'll talk about what I find most useful—and why, of course!

SEED BEADS

Where would we be without these wonderful tiny bits of glass we call seed beads? As the primary component of just about everything I make, seed beads are the staple of my supply lists. In my stash, you'll find various sizes of round seed beads, from 15/0 to 6/0, but the majority are 11/0 and 15/0. When I first started beading, I shopped at the local craft chain store, buying the inexpensive beads I found there. Over time, however, I discovered the Japanese seed beads that my local bead stores sold, and the quality, colors and consistency of these beads quickly won me over.

Many of my designs are geometric or rely heavily on symmetry, so I definitely prefer to use consistently shaped seed beads. Cylinder beads are the most regular, and their shape makes them perfect to use in peyote- or brick-stitch projects. I don't have quite as many of these beauties in stock as I'd like. What I have the most of are the relatively new Permanent Finish (TOHO) and Duracoat (Miyuki) seed beads. The coating on these seed beads will not rub off with wear and use, unlike their cheaper galvanized counterparts (see the Bead Finishes sidebar). A large number of colors are available; I have many in both size 15/0 and 11/0. They are also made in matte colors, which I love to throw in to add contrast and dimension to a bead-woven piece.

SHAPED BEADS

Besides round seed beads, another type of bead I keep in my inventory is shaped beads. Many of them are two-hole beads, such as SuperDuos and twins, Tila and half-Tila, bricks, daggers and lentils. I also like teeny-tiny cubes, triangle beads, bugle

Bead Finishes

People who have very acidic skin may still have problems with the coating coming off of Permanent Finish and Duracoat beads, but this is uncommon. I recommend you test any coating/finish or dyed bead for stability before using it.

You should also avoid wearing perfume or lotion with your bead-woven jewelry, as these can cause damage to the beads and thread.

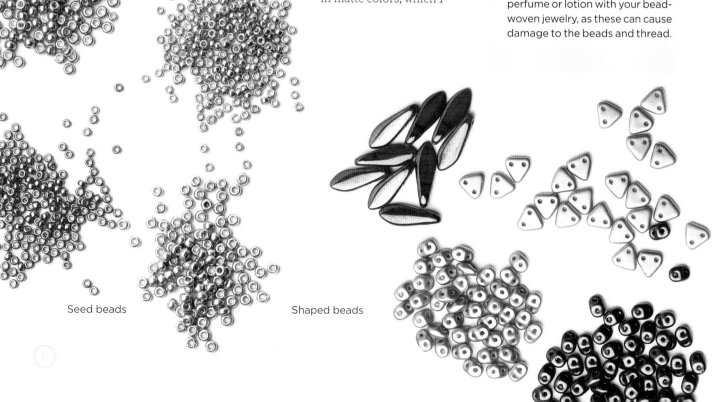

Seed beads

Shaped beads

beads and drops. By substituting different shapes into designs with the same stitches, you can create completely different looks.

PEARLS

I have lots of glass pearls in sizes ranging from 2mm to 10mm. I have primarily round pearls, which are my favorites, but I also like oval and disk pearls. Pearls make a nice base upon which to embellish with seed beads and crystals.

CRYSTALS

If I had to choose only one type of bead to use for embellishment, I would have to choose bicone crystals. The great thing about bicones is their shape lets them nestle in where a round bead may not fit without showing thread. I sometimes like to substitute faceted fire-polished glass beads for bicones; they're not crystals, but they still have a lot of sparkle.

RIVOLIS AND CABOCHONS

Rivolis and Lunasoft cabochons are my go-to for pendants and other focal objects. One thing I really like about the Luna cabs is that they're flat on the back rather than pointed like the rivolis. This allows me to put two of them back-to-back to create a reversible piece. Two for the price (or at least the stitching time) of one!

NEEDLES AND THREAD

I use size 12 or 13 needles, depending on the project. Most of the time I use size 12 sharps. The fact that they're short makes them easier to get into tight spaces. I keep size 13 needles handy in case I need to go through a bead with a small hole or one that's already filled with thread.

When I first started beading, my more experienced beader friends recommended that I use fishing line instead of beading thread. Since then I have used many different types of thread, but I still prefer 6lb. FireLine, a type of fishing line, for most of my work. Because I use a lot of crystals, which have sharp holes, braided and/or fused line holds up quite well without breaking. I rarely double my thread, and I never use wax or conditioner. As for color, I usually use smoke unless the beads I'm using are transparent, and then I'll use crystal.

Pearls

Pointed-back crystals

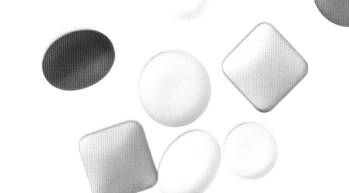

Lunasoft cabochons

Clasps

CLASPS

While I do sometimes make beaded clasps to customize a piece, most of the time I use a metal clasp. My favorite clasps are two-hole magnetic fold-over clasps, slider clasps, trailer hitch (ball-and-socket) clasps, magnetic clasps and toggles. Attaching clasps with jump rings makes it easy to adjust the size of a piece. Using a thread guard, instead of attaching the jump rings directly to the beadwork, can help reduce friction on the beads and thread as well.

TOOLS

My favorite tools to keep within arm's reach at all times are my scissors (kids' scissors actually cut FireLine easily), thread burner (for removing threads when scissors can't cut close enough to the work), triangle scoop and two pairs of pliers (for opening and closing jump rings).

STORAGE

My storage system is ever evolving, but one thing that I can't live without is my SeeMore Beads bag. What I love about this bag is that it hangs over the top of a door, so the beads I use most are in plain view and easy to reach. I also travel a lot and prefer to take as many beads with me as possible, so the travel bag is perfect. As for bead containers, I am slowly moving my seed-bead inventory to rectangular flip-top tubes. They're large and don't roll around like round tubes do.

Beadweaver's Tool Kit

In addition to the specific supplies listed for each project in this book, you'll want to have the following general materials and tools on hand as well:

– beading needles
– thread (Fireline recommended)
– thread burner
– scissors
– 2 pairs of pliers

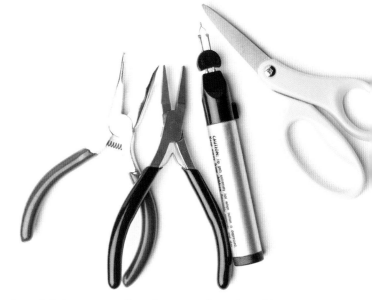
From left: bent-nose pliers, flat-nose pliers, thread burner, children's scissors

Needles and thread (with thread burner)

My Favorite Stitches

The first off-loom beadweaving stitch I ever learned was flat peyote. I saw a flower pattern in a book and thought it looked simple enough, so I tried it. I moved on to other stitches soon after that and quickly discovered my passion for beadweaving. In this section, you'll learn a few of the stitches I use most often.

HERRINGBONE STITCH

The first stitch I learned after peyote was herringbone. It can be made in a variety of ways: flat, circular or tubular. In this section, I will show two of the three methods: flat and basic tubular. While I sometimes use circular in my work, I won't show it here because it's not included in the projects in this book.

Flat Herringbone

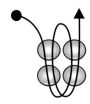

1 Pick up 4 color A 11/0 beads and pass through them all again, manipulating them if needed so that there are 2 stacks of 2 beads next to each other.

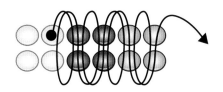

2 Pick up 2 color B beads and pass through the last stack in the base. Pass through the new beads again. Repeat this step until all stacks are added. Each stack will be connected to the adjacent stacks on both ends.

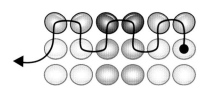

3 Once the ladder base is built, begin adding rows of standard herringbone. Pick up 2 beads and pass down through the top bead of the next stack. Pass up through the top bead in the next stack. Repeat this step across the row. Stop after passing down through the top bead in the last stack.

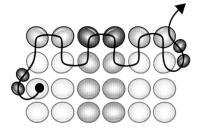

4 To step up, pick up one or two 15/0 seed beads, pass the thread around the bead being exited in the previous step and through the last bead added in the top row. Continue working in regular herringbone to add a new row and then step up again.

Bead Sizing Issues

All beads are not created equal! A different manufacturer will likely mean a slightly different-size bead, even if both are marked as the same size. Different coatings can change the size of the bead as well. If the counts given in the pattern don't seem to be working, you may want to try using a different brand of bead, a different finish, or (as a last resort) a different count of beads altogether.

Faux Ribbon Pendant, page 114

Tubular Herringbone

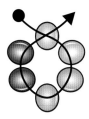

1 On a comfortable length of thread, string 2 color A, 2 color B, and 2 color C beads for round 1. Pass the needle through the first bead again, forming a circle. Leave a 6" (15cm) tail. Don't tie a knot.

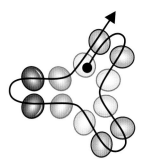

2 For round 2, pick up 2A and pass down through the next A in the round. Pass up through the next B. Pick up 2B and pass down through the next B in the round. Pass up through the next C. Pick up 2C and pass down through the next C.

3 Step up by passing up through the adjacent A and the first A added in the previous step.

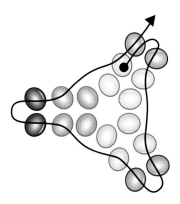

4 For all subsequent rounds, repeat the last 2 steps until the tube is the desired length.

5 Remove the tail thread from the first 5 beads if desired.

— TIP —

When making a tubular herringbone rope, remember to step up at the end of each round. Not doing so will result in a kink in your rope.

A free tutorial for twisted tubular herringbone can be found on my website beadingbutterfly.com.

RIGHT ANGLE WEAVE (RAW)

Right angle weave is a very popular stitch and is used by many of the most well-known international bead designers. Though RAW can be difficult to learn, it can be quite useful once you understand the basic structure for the stitch. It lends itself to easy shaping by changing bead counts or sizes.

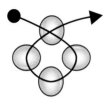

1 Pick up 4 beads and pass through the first bead again to form the first unit.

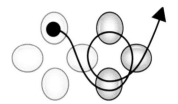

2 To add a unit in a straight, single row, exit the edge bead upon which the new unit is to be built. Pick up 3 new beads and pass through the bead being exited. Continue around the new unit to the desired point.

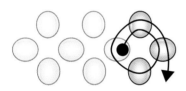

3 Repeat the previous step to add units.

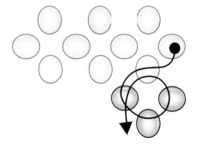

4 To change directions, weave to the side desired and repeat step 1 to add a new unit.

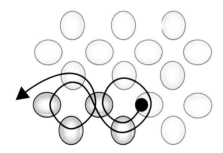

5 When adding subsequent units to subsequent rows, you need to pick up only 2 beads to complete the unit because the other 2 beads are already in place.

— TIP —

If you have difficulty learning RAW with seed beads, try using bugle beads instead.

CUBIC RIGHT ANGLE WEAVE (CRAW)

In cubic right angle weave, the resulting units are, as the name implies, cubes. The beads sit next to each other as if they are on the cube's edges, rather than on the face or corner.

Pearl Cross necklace, in the gallery

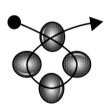

1 For the base, pick up 4 beads and pass through the first bead again.

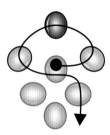

2 For side 1, pick up 3 beads and pass through the bead being exited. Pass through the next bead in the base.

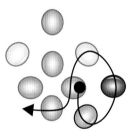

3 For side 2, pick up 2 beads and pass down through the adjacent bead from side 1. Pass through the next 2 beads in the base.

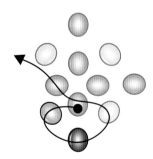

4 For side 3, repeat the previous step.

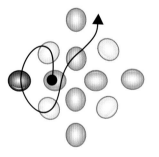

5 For side 4, pass through the adjacent bead from side 1. Pick up 1 bead and pass through the adjacent bead from side 3. Pass through the next 2 beads in the base.

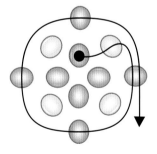

6 Pass up through the adjacent bead in the next side and through the top bead in the side. Pass through the 4 beads on the top of the cube. These 4 beads are now the base of the next unit.

7 Repeat steps 2–6 as many times as desired.

PEYOTE STITCH

Peyote stitch was the first stitch I learned. It was an even-count design, so it wasn't too difficult, but unfortunately, many designs call for an odd count for symmetry. Fortunately, with a little practice, odd-count peyote can also become second nature.

Even-Count Peyote

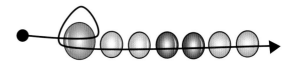

1 Put a stop bead on your thread. Pick up the beads for the first 2 rows.

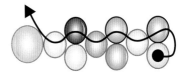

2 For row 3, turn around. Pick up a bead, skip a bead and pass through the next bead. Repeat to the end of the row.

You can take the stop bead off at any time now that the initial rows are secure.

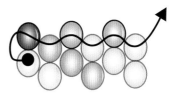

3 For row 4, turn around. Pick up a bead and pass through the next up bead. Repeat to the end of the row.

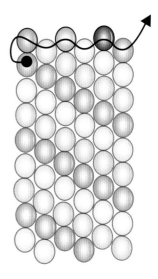

4 Repeat step 3 as many times as desired.

Kiss Me Quick bracelet, with Peyote toggle, page 124

15

Odd-Count Peyote

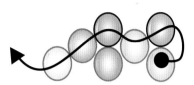

1 Stitch the first 3 rows using the instructions for even-count peyote. There is no bead to stitch into in order to add the last bead of the row. Instead of adding the new bead, continue down through the last bead of the first row.

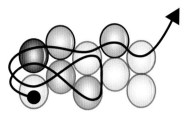

2 Pick up the bead that you skipped in the top row. Pass through the last bead in the previous row. Continue through the next bead diagonally. Turn around and weave through the next bead directly above and 2 more diagonally down. Pass back through the bead added at the beginning of this step and you are now ready to add the next row as you normally would.

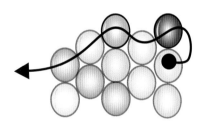

3 Add the next row in the usual way until you reach the end of the row. Instead of picking up the last bead, pass down through the last bead in the lower row.

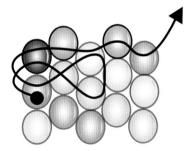

4 Repeat step 2 to add the missing bead and do another figure eight to turn around. Add the next row normally.
   Repeat the last 2 steps until the strip is the desired length.

ST. PETERSBURG STITCH

St. Petersburg stitch can be used in a single or double row, depending on your desired look. The double-row version has a shared "spine" bead.

Firewheel Daisy necklace strap, page 68

Single Row

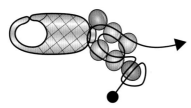

1 Pick up 1 color B bead and pass through the bead again. Pick up 4 color A beads and pass through the first 2A again. Pick up 1 of the lobster-claw clasps and 1B. Pass through the second 2A again. Pass through the A beads and clasp a couple of times to secure, exiting from the A shown in the diagram.

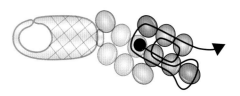

2 Pick up 4A and pass through the first 2A you just picked up again. Pick up 1B (this is a stop-stitch bead) and pass back through 3A. Pick up 1B (this side of the strip is the "turn" edge) and pass through the next 2A.

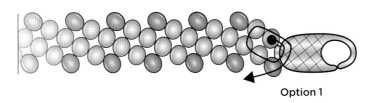

Option 1

3 Repeat step 2 until the strap is the desired length. Pick up the second lobster clasp (option 1) or 2B (option 2). Pass through the adjacent B and the last 4A you picked up. Retrace the path a couple of times to secure. Weave in your threads, secure with a half-hitch knot and trim the threads. If you did not add a second lobster clasp, insert a jump ring in the space between the A and B beads at the end of the strap. If you are using 2 clasps, attach both to a jump ring to close the bracelet.

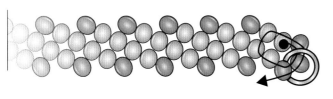

Option 2

— TIP —

Use 11/0 beads to complete a St. Petersburg-stitch bracelet as shown in these steps.

Double Row

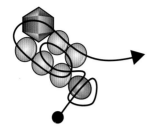

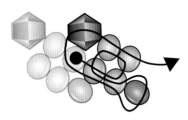

1 Pick up 1 color B and pass through the bead again. Pick up 4 color A and pass through the first 2A again. Pick up 1A and 1 bead C. Pass through the second 2A again.

2 Pick up 4A and pass through the first 2A you just picked up again. Pick up 1B and pass back through 3A. Pick up 1C and pass through the next 2A.

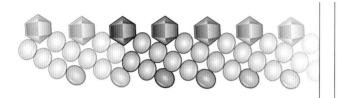

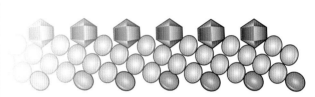

3 Repeat the previous step until the strip is the desired length. Weave in your threads and trim.

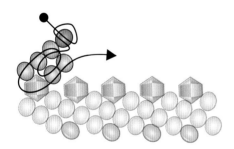

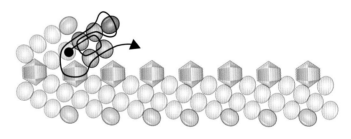

4 On a new piece of thread, repeat step 1 of this section. However, instead of picking up a new C, pass through the first C from the existing work.

5 Repeat step 2 of this section. Again, pass through the next C in the existing work instead of picking up a new C.

— **TIP** —

Use 11/0 beads for A and B and 3mm crystals for C to make a double-row bracelet following the steps on this page.

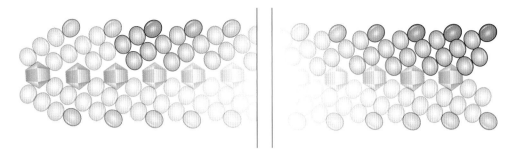

6 Repeat step 5 down the length of the strap.

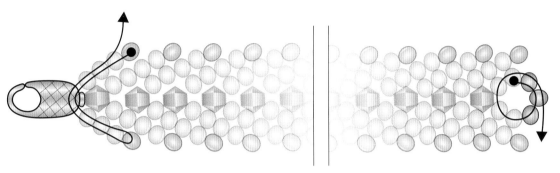

7 Add a clasp to 1 or both ends of the bracelet. If only 1 clasp is used, add a loop of seed beads to 1 end and attach a jump ring to the loop. If you are using 2 clasps, pick up 1A, the clasp, and 1A (not shown in diagram). Pass through all of the beads added in this step several times to secure. Follow the left side of the diagram to secure the second clasp. Weave in your threads, secure with a half-hitch knot, and trim the threads.

Adding Thread

I use a couple of different methods to add thread. My primary method is to use a weaver's knot, which I originally learned from Carol Wilcox Wells's book *The Art and Elegance of Beadweaving*. Videos describing this knot can be found online, but basically you tie the new thread onto the old thread and just keep right on stitching as if you never added new thread to begin with. If this method doesn't work for whatever reason (FireLine Crystal is hard to knot because of how slippery it is, for instance, and sometimes a knot is too big to fit through a bead hole), you can just add a new thread farther back in the work, weave to your new location, and keep stitching. After you are done, you will need to weave in the old thread and the tail of the new one.

Terms to Remember

STEP UP: A step up is sometimes required to maneuver your thread to the appropriate location in order to start a new row or round after the previous row or round has been completed.

HALF-HITCH KNOT: A half-hitch knot is created by wrapping the thread around another thread, leaving a small loop. Stitch through the loop before tightening the thread, thereby securing the thread.

STOP BEAD: A bead that is placed on the tail end of the thread to keep the first beads from falling off until they are secured to the rest of the work. Stop beads will be removed.

UP BEAD: In some stitches, particularly peyote, the work will have some beads that stick up away from the rest of the work. These are up beads.

ZIP UP: When two edges of beadwork contain up beads, you can use peyote stitch to zip them together. Stitch through alternating up beads from each edge. The two edges will close up like a zipper.

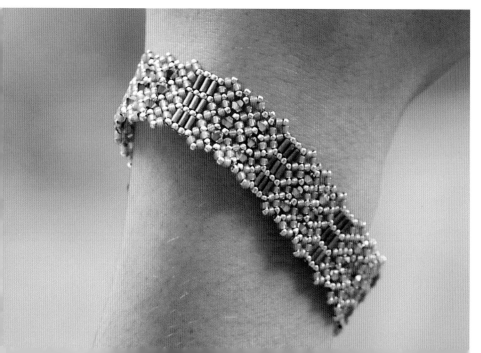

Chapter One

Double Diamond Right Angle Weave

I was a slow convert to right angle weave. I watched my friends go nuts over RAW, and I read other designers' blog posts about how great and versatile a stitch it is. For some reason, I never really caught the bug. But one day, while playing around with tiny cubes and seed beads, I finally got it. The cubes I used helped my RAW units to keep their square, angled shape, and it was that shape that intrigued me.

As I learned more about RAW and what could be done with it, I realized that even more than those little units of squares, I loved making diamonds. It wasn't as simple as making the sides of the units bigger, although doing so does give a similar look. What I wanted was sharp angles; I discovered that a second pass, to add beads in the corners of the inside unit, was all I needed to get the shape I desired.

Double Diamond Right Angle Weave (DDRAW) Primer

DDRAW is very similar to basic RAW in that each unit is stitched in a square, and you will change direction with each unit. The main difference, however, is that with DDRAW you will make two passes around each unit before moving on to the next.

To learn DDRAW, start with two colors of seed beads. You can experiment with different-size beads, but most of the projects in this book are made with 11/0 seed beads. Each DDRAW unit has eight beads (one outer corner bead is shared with an adjacent unit) and two trips around the unit (one to add the inner beads and a second to add the outer corner beads).

Use this method to make your DDRAW strip as wide and as long as needed. Corner beads from the second pass will be used to connect each unit, and you will need to create the inner ring of beads before adding the outer corner beads. Each unit (once the inner and outer beads are in place) will change stitching directions. If you make a unit and are stitching clockwise, the adjacent unit will be stitched counterclockwise.

Queen of Diamonds bracelet (page 28)

MAKING THE FIRST ROW

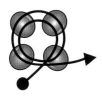

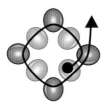

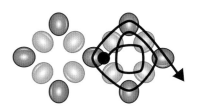

1 On a comfortable length of thread, string 4 color A seed beads. Pass through the first A to make a square. Pass through all 4 beads again and pull snugly on the tail and working threads to tighten.

2 Pick up 1 color B seed bead. Pass through the next A in the previous round. Repeat 3 times. Pass through the first B. This is a single unit of DDRAW.

3 Pick up 4A. Pass through the first A, keeping the new square as close to the existing work as possible. Pick up 1B and pass through the next A in the inner square just formed. Repeat twice more. Pass through the next 5 beads in the outer row of this diamond to exit the B on the opposite side of the starting point of this step.

ADDING SUBSEQUENT ROWS

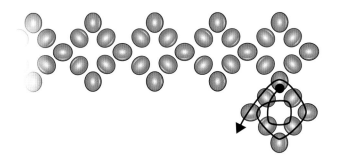

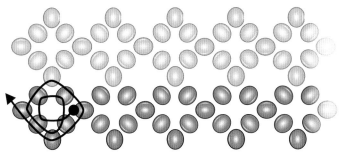

4 Repeat step 3 until the strip is the desired length. Continue through 2 more beads in the last diamond. Repeat step 3 one more time, but stop when your thread is exiting the bead shown in the diagram.

5 Pick up 4A. Pass through the first A, keeping the square as close to the existing work as possible. Pick up 1B and pass through the next A in the inner square. Repeat once. Pass through the nearest B in the diamond from the first row. Pass through the next 6 beads in the diamond to exit the second B added in this step.

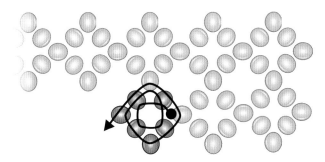

6 Pick up 4A. Pass through the first A to make a square. Pass through the nearest B from the diamond in the first row. Pass through the next A, pick up 1B, pass through the next A, pick up 1B and pass through the next 6 beads in the diamond to exit the first B added in this step.

7 Repeat steps 5 and 6 until the second row of the strip is complete.

In *Trapeze,* page 36, Superduos and crystals are used to shape a base strip of DDRAW.

Palisades

One of the first things I do when I play with a new stitch is to add another type of bead into the mix. After making a short strip of DDRAW, I noticed that a 3mm bicone would fit perfectly in the space between the corner beads from one unit to the next. I also like to see if another type of stitch can be started from a piece of existing work. I have a stash of 3mm bugle beads, and since they also fit perfectly in the space between DDRAW units, I thought a small section of peyote would be a nice contrast to the DDRAW. The resulting piece is reminiscent of a castle wall, thus the name *Palisades*.

MATERIALS

4 grams 11/0 silver-lined salmon seed beads (A)

2 grams 15/0 Duracoat gold seed beads (B)

48 jet AB2X bicones, 3mm

1 gram matte green iris bugle beads, 3mm

1 copper 2-hole slide clasp

2 copper jump rings, 6mm

SIZE

Makes a bracelet about 7¼" (18.5cm) long

This alternate colorway uses seafoam and silver seed beads, metallic blue bicones and matte jet iris bugle beads.

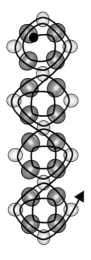

1 To start the first motif of DDRAW and crystals, make a strip of DDRAW 4 units long (see pages 22–23 for basic DDRAW instructions). Use 11/0 (color A) beads for the inner pass and 15/0 (color B) beads for the outer pass. Exit a side outer bead headed toward the center of the strip.

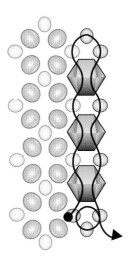

2 Pick up a crystal and pass through the outer B in the next unit. Repeat twice. Pick up 2B and pass back through the last crystal picked up. Pick up 1B and pass through the next crystal. Repeat once. Pick up 2B, pass through the adjacent B in the direction of the last crystal but do not go through the crystal. Pass through the first of the last 2B you just picked up, next to the crystal, exiting away from the work.

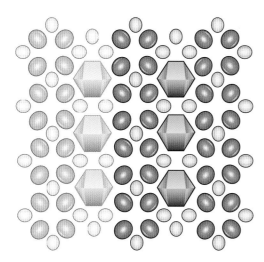

3 Build another row of DDRAW off of the B beads added in the last step (refer to the instructions for adding subsequent rows on page 23). Add another row of crystals by repeating step 2 and then add a final row of DDRAW off of the B beads you just added.

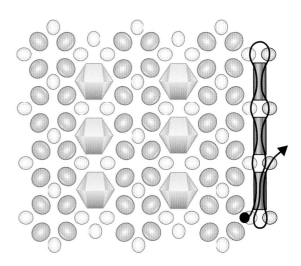

4 Create a peyote stitch connection with bugle beads. For peyote rows 1 and 2, pick up a bugle and pass through the B in the next unit. Repeat twice. Pick up 1B, turn around and pass back through the last bugle picked up. Add 2 more B in this manner and pass back through the last B (the one being exited at the beginning of this step). Pick up 1B and turn around, passing through the first bugle picked up in this row and the next B.

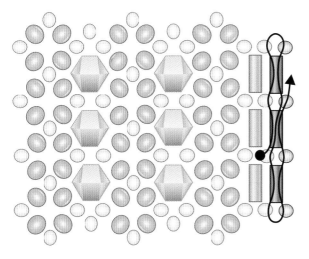

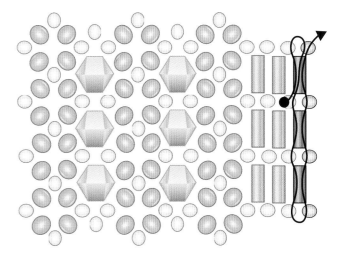

5 For peyote rows 3 and 4, pick up a bugle and pass through the next B. Repeat once. Pick up 1B, turn around and pass back through the last bugle you picked up. Pick up 1B and pass through the first bugle you picked up in this step. Pass through the next B. Pick up a bugle and pass through the end B. Pick up 1B, turn around and pass through the bugle. Pick up 1B and pass through the next bugle and the next B.

6 For peyote rows 5 and 6, pick up a bugle and pass through the next B. Pick up 1B, turn around and pass back through the bugle you just picked up and the next B. Pick up a bugle and pass through the next B. Repeat once. Pick up 1B, turn around and pass back through the last bugle. Pick up 1B and pass through the next bugle. Repeat. Pass through the last B.

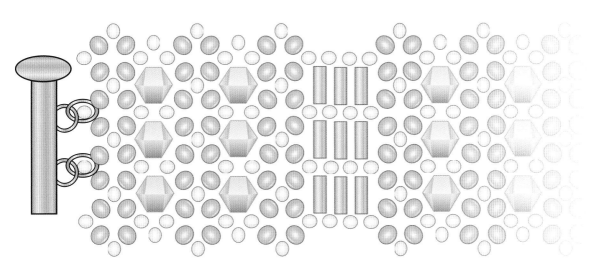

7 To finish, continue adding DDRAW and crystal motifs separated by peyote-stitched bugle bead connections until the bracelet is the desired length. Stop after a row of DDRAW. Weave in your threads, secure with half-hitch knots and trim. To add the clasp, insert a jump ring into each of the 2 center DDRAW units on either end of the bracelet and attach them to the clasp rings.

— TIP FOR LEFTIES—

If you are making a flat piece of beadwork, sometimes all you need to do is turn the pattern upside down. As a leftie myself, I find it easier to stitch to the left instead of the right as many patterns are drawn.

Queen of Diamonds

The next variation I like to try with a stitch is a change in direction. I ask myself, "What happens if I extend the stitch vertically instead of horizontally (or vice versa)?" After making *Palisades* (page 24), I wanted the next design to use pearls instead of crystals. I simplified the pattern from three rows of DDRAW to only two and eliminated the peyote stitch completely, making the single row of pearls the focus. The original colorway of steel, wine, and purple is characteristic of royalty, something a queen might wear.

MATERIALS
3 grams 11/0 Permanent Finish steel seed beads (A)

3 grams 11/0 Permanent Finish wine seed beads (B)

30 purple glass pearls, 3mm

1 silver 2-hole magnetic fold-over clasp

SIZE
Makes a bracelet about 6¾" (17cm) long

A colorway of gilt lined and transparent seed beads gives this bracelet a soft romantic look.

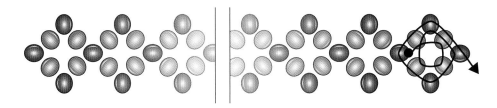

1 Make a strip of DDRAW (see pages 22–23 for basic DDRAW instructions) until the strip is the desired bracelet length minus 1" (2.5cm). The inner beads will be 11/0 A beads and the outer beads will be 11/0 B beads.

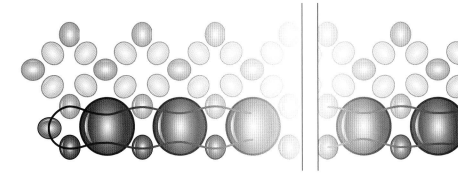

2 To add the center row of pearls, continue through the next 2 beads in the last unit, pick up a pearl and pass through the outer B in the next unit. Continue adding pearls in this manner until you reach the other end of the bracelet. Pick up 1A and 1B. Pass back through the pearl. Pick up 1B and pass through the next pearl. Repeat to the other end of the bracelet. After you exit the last pearl, pick up 1B and 1A. Pass through the adjacent B, moving toward the pearl but not into the pearl. Pass through the last B added again.

— TIP —

It is important to maintain a loose to medium tension while stitching this piece so that it will lie flat. Stitching too tightly could result in buckling.

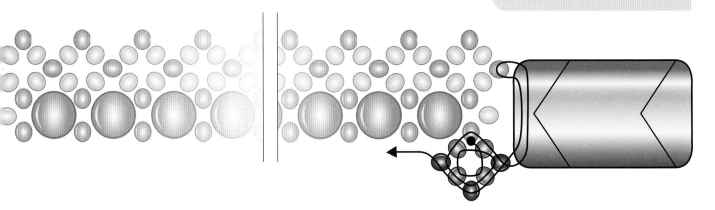

3 To add the first half of the clasp, pick up 4A. Pass through the first A forming a square. Pick up 1B and pass through the next A in the square. Repeat twice. Pass through the next B, A and B. *Pass through both holes of the clasp, through the B on the opposite side, back through both holes of the clasp and through the adjacent B again (pass toward the outer edge of the piece).* Retrace the thread path between * and * 2 or 3 times for added security. Pass through the next 4 beads to exit the last B added in this step.

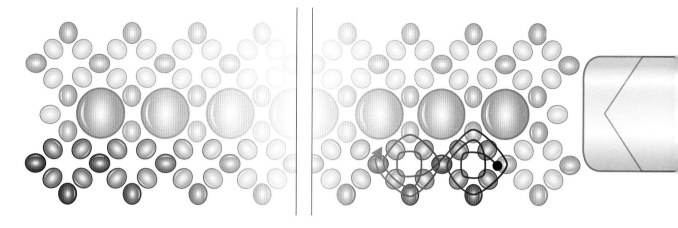

4 Using the basic DDRAW instructions from pages 22–23, complete a second row of DDRAW units down the entire length of the bracelet; this is the last row.

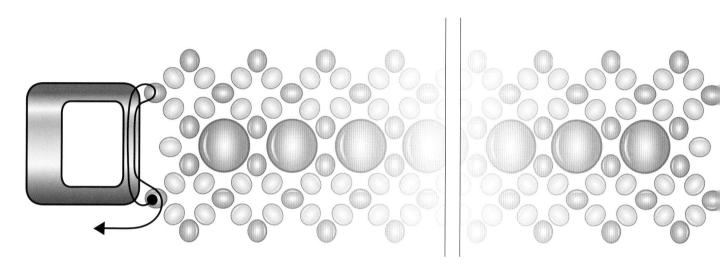

5 When you get to the end of side 2, continue around the diamond until your thread is coming out of the B at the end of the bracelet. To add the second half of the clasp, *pass through both holes of the clasp, through the B on the opposite side of the bracelet, back through both holes of the clasp and through the adjacent B again.* Retrace the thread path between * and * 2 or 3 times for added security. Weave in your working and tail threads, tie a few half-hitch knots to secure, and trim the threads.

Dainty Lace

Bracelets are nice, but what about necklaces? Up to this point, both pieces I had designed with DDRAW were very straight. I wondered how I could change it up to make a necklace that would curve comfortably around the neck. My solution was based on the fact that the connections between units are single seed beads. These connections would be flexible enough to curve. I didn't want to just have a single row of DDRAW, though. That would be boring. So I thought back to *Palisades* (page 24) and decided that I could use small rectangular "tabs" as focal motifs for the necklace.

MATERIALS

3 grams 11/0 frosted amythest berry seed beads (A)

3 grams 11/0 Permanent Finish silver seed beads (B)

14 orchid glass pearls, 3mm

20 pastel lilac SuperDuo 2-hole beads (SD), 2.5mm × 5mm

1 silver ball-and-socket clasp

2 silver jump rings, 6mm

SIZE

Makes a necklace 18½" (47cm) long

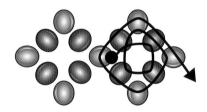

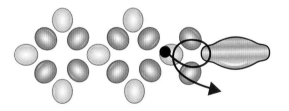

1 First, you'll make a strap of DDRAW, encircled SuperDuos (ESD) and encircled pearls (EP). To start, make 2 units of DDRAW (see pages 22–23 for basic DDRAW instructions) using A beads for the inner pass and B beads for the outer pass. Weave around the second unit to exit the B on the opposite side of the starting point.

2 To start unit 3 (encircled SuperDuo [ESD]), pick up 1A, 1SD and 1A. Pass through the adjacent B and the first A again.

— TIP —

SuperDuos can sometimes have clogged holes, so make sure that both holes are open before using each one.

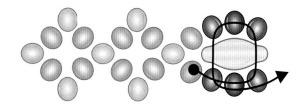

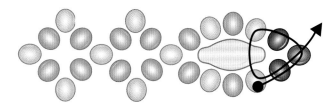

3 Pick up 1B, 1A and 1B. Pass through the second hole of the SD and pick up 1B, 1A and 1B. Pass through the first hole of the SD and the first 3 beads picked up in this step.

4 Pick up 1A, 1B and 1A. Pass around the end of the SD and through the B on the other side. Pass through the second hole of the SD, the adjacent B, and the next A and B.

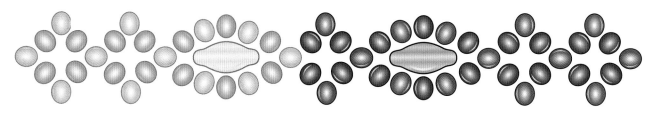

5 Add 1 unit of DDRAW, 1 ESD unit (steps 2–4) and 2 units of DDRAW; these are units 4–7.

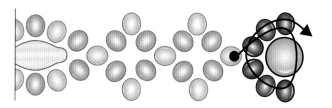

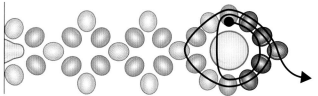

6 For unit 8 (encircled pearl [EP]), pick up 1A, 1B, 1A, a pearl, 1A, 1B and 1A. Pass through the first 3 beads picked up.

7 Pick up 1B, 2A and 1B. Pass through the A on the other side of the pearl, through the pearl, through the adjacent A and through the first 2 beads you picked up in this step. Pick up 1B and pass through the second 2 beads you picked up in this step. Pass through the rest of the beads around the pearl, making sure that you pass through the corner B from the previous DDRAW unit. Exit the B on the end of the new EP unit.

8 Continue adding units to your strap, following the pattern shown, ending with a DDRAW unit just prior to adding the third EP unit. End this step with your thread exiting a side B and heading away from the existing work.

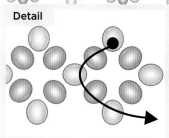

Detail

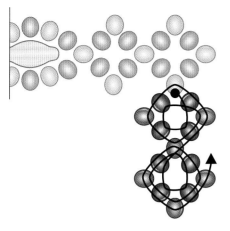

9 To add the pearl tab, add 2 units of DDRAW from the side of the last DDRAW unit. Continue around to the B on the side of the last unit, headed back toward the rest of the work.

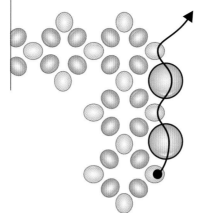

10 Pick up a pearl and pass through the B on the next DDRAW unit. Repeat once more.

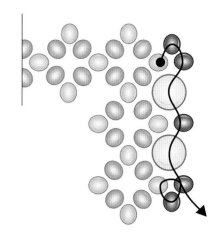

11 Pick up 2B and pass back through the last pearl added. Pick up 1B and pass through the next pearl. Pick up 2B and pass through the adjacent B toward the pearl but do not go through the pearl. Pass through the next-to-last B you picked up.

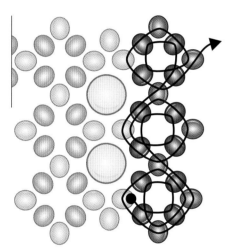

12 Add 3 units of DDRAW along the new edge, building from the new B beads from the previous step.

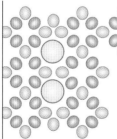

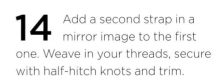

13 Add 6 more units: DDRAW, ESD, DDRAW, ESD and 2 DDRAW. Then follow steps 9–12 to add another pearl tab. Repeat this entire step 3 more times until you have 5 pearl tabs.

14 Add a second strap in a mirror image to the first one. Weave in your threads, secure with half-hitch knots and trim.

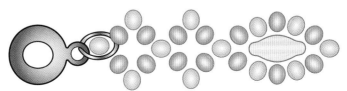

15 To finish, add a jump ring to the end DDRAW unit on each strap and connect it to one half of the clasp. Repeat on the other side.

Trapeze

The open spaces between two strips of DDRAW are perfect for 3mm pearls or crystals. So the next thing I ask myself is, "What if I use 4mm crystals in the spaces instead?" By filling the space with a larger bead, the work will curve. Once that happens, what can I do with that new shape? By folding the strip in half and connecting the two sides with SuperDuos, I get a shape that is both playful and elegant. Even more exciting, it can be adapted for both earrings and necklaces.

MATERIALS

1 gram 15/0 Permanent Finish silver seed beads (A) (optional)

1 gram 11/0 Permanent Finish silver seed beads (B)

1 gram 11/0 Permanent Finish turquoise seed beads (C)

20 jet AB2X bicone crystals (D), 3mm

14 jet AB2X bicone crystals (E), 4mm

14 crystal vitrail SuperDuo 2-hole beads (SD), 2.5mm × 5mm

2 thread guards

2 ear wires

As an alternative, use only A beads instead of the B and C beads in step 5.

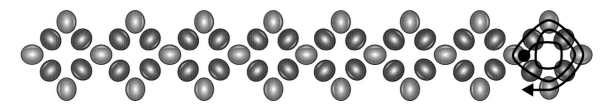

1 Make a strip of DDRAW (see pages 22–23 for basic DDRAW instructions) 8 units long with B beads in the inner pass and C beads in the outer pass. Continue around the last unit until you exit the side bead as shown. You should be headed toward the rest of the work.

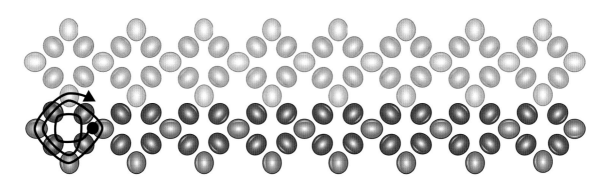

2 Add a second row of DDRAW to the first (see Adding Subsequent Rows on page 23). Continue around the last unit to the connecting bead between the 2 rows. You should be headed toward the rest of the work.

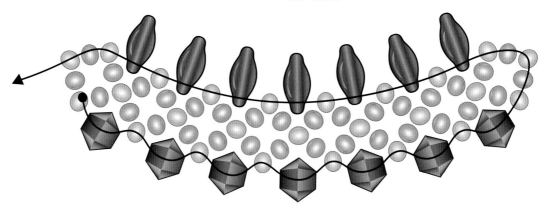

3 Fold the 2 sides of the strip and push them together. The center beads become the beads at the bottom of the curve. Pick up 1E and pass through the next C at the bottom of the strip. Repeat 6 more times. Maintain very firm tension, and the strip will start to curve naturally as the crystals are added. Pass through the next 4 beads around the end of the row. Pick up 1SD and pass through the next C. Repeat 6 more times. Again, maintain firm tension to help the piece keep a curve. Continue through the next 2 beads to exit the C at the end of the strip.

— TIP —

Be careful not to pull your thread at an angle when exiting a crystal because you could cut your thread. Always pull out parallel to the crystal's hole.

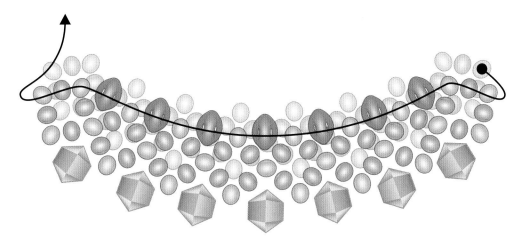

4 Flip your work over. Pass up through the adjacent C on what is now the front side of the strip and through 2 more beads. Pass through the second hole of the last SD picked up in the previous step and the next C. Repeat 6 more times until all SDs are attached on both sides. Continue through the next 2 beads and then pass up through the adjacent C on the other side of the strip.

5 String 1D, 1C, 1B and 1C 5 times. String a thread guard. String 1C, 1B, 1C and 1D 5 times. Pass through one of the Cs at the other end of the curve and up through the adjacent C. Go back through all of the beads and the thread guard again and down through the C adjacent to where the thread was exiting at the beginning of this step. Weave your threads into the work, secure with half-hitch knots and trim the thread. Add an ear wire to the thread guard at the top of the earring. Repeat to make a second earring.

To make a smaller pair of earrings, make the base only 6 units long instead of 8. For an even more delicate look, pass back through the top crystal in the seed-bead chain instead of picking up a new one on the second side.

Le Petit Trapèze

After making several variations of the original *Trapeze* (page 36), I decided to make a daintier version with 15/0 seed beads instead of 11/0. For dramatic effect, I added some daggers to the bottom of the motif. The earring is made following the directions for the original; the only difference is that the curve was not as pronounced, so you have to tug the thread tightly as you add the SuperDuos.

MATERIALS

1 gram 15/0 Permanent Finish gold seed beads (A)

1 gram 15/0 Permanent Finish saffron seed beads (B)

1 gram 15/0 silver-lined turquoise seed beads (C)

8 turquoise AB2X bicone crystals (D), 3mm

14 aqua vitrail SuperDuo 2-hole beads (SD), 2.5mm × 5mm

10 peacock daggers, 5mm × 16mm

2 copper thread guards

2 copper ear wires

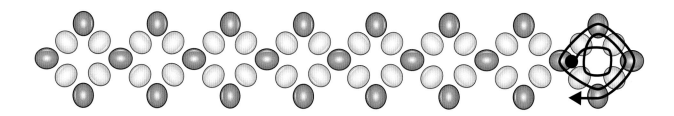

1 Make a strip of DDRAW (see pages 22–23 for basic DDRAW instructions) that is 8 units long with A beads in the inner pass and B beads in the outer pass. Continue around the last unit until you exit the side bead as shown. You should be headed toward the rest of the work.

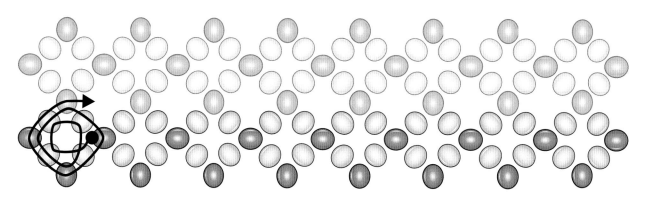

2 Add a second row of DDRAW to the first (see Adding Subsequent Rows on page 23). Continue around the last unit to the connecting bead between the 2 rows. You should be headed toward the rest of the work.

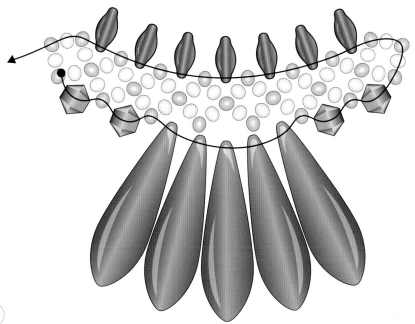

3 Fold the 2 sides of the strip and push them together. Pick up 1D and pass through the next B at the bottom of the strip. Repeat once. Pick up 5 daggers, skip 2B and pass through the next B. Pick up 1D and pass through the next B. Repeat once. Maintain very firm tension so that the strip will curve. Pass through the next 4 beads around the end of the row. Pick up 1SD and pass through the next B. Repeat 6 more times. Again, maintain firm tension so that a curve forms. Continue through the next 2 beads to exit the B at the end of the strip.

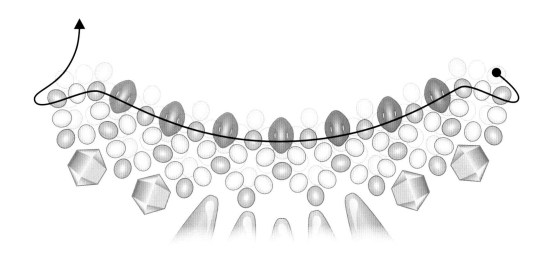

4 Flip your work over. Pass up through the B on what is now the front side of the strip and through 2 more beads. Pass through the second hole of the last SD and the next B. Repeat 6 more times until all SDs are attached on both sides. Continue through the next 2 beads and then pass up through the B on the other side of the strip.

— TIP —

If the motif is not curving as much as you like, retrace your thread path through the SuperDuos, maintaining very firm tension and creating the curve with your hands as you do so.

5 String 1C, 1A, 1B and 1A 5 times. String 1C and 1A. String a thread guard. String 1A, 1C, 1A and 1B 5 times. Pick up 1A and 1C. Pass through 1 of the B at the other end of the motif and up through the B on the other side. Go back through all of the beads again and down through the B adjacent to where the thread was exiting at the beginning of this step. Weave your threads into the work, tie a few half-hitch knots and trim the thread. Add an ear wire to the thread guard at the top of the earring. Repeat to make a second earring.

Starflower

Whenever I work on a new stitch or obsess over a new shape, I invariably try to figure out if I can turn it into a bezel of some kind. I love crystals, particularly rivolis, and the bigger the better. As I played around with *Trapeze* (page 36), I realized that if I didn't close up the inside edge with SuperDuos, I could make a longer strip and wrap it around a crystal stone. The hard part was finding the right bead counts and sizes to fit.

MATERIALS FOR
PENDANT ONLY

1 gram 15/0 Duracoat gold seed beads (A)

2 grams 11/0 matte metallic sage luster seed beads (B)

2 grams 11/0 Duracoat gold seed beads (C)

17 light cremerose glass pearls (D), 3mm

8 rose luster SuperDuo 2-hole beads (SD), 2.5mm × 5mm

1 purple haze crystal pointed-back stone, 27mm

SIZE
Makes a pendant 1½″ (4cm) in diameter

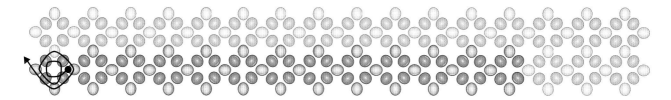

1 Start by creating the bezel. Make a strip of DDRAW (see pages 22–23 for basic DDRAW instructions) 2 units wide and 16 units long with B beads in the inner pass and C beads in the outer pass.

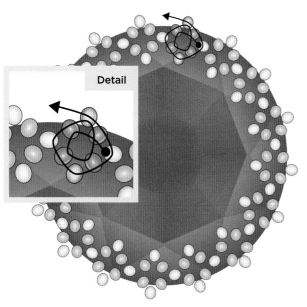

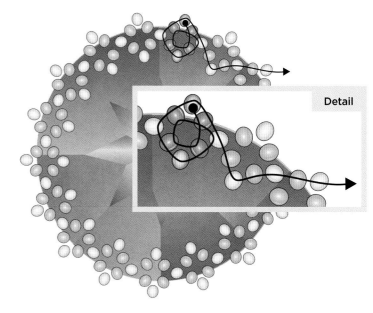

2 Add a seventeenth unit to 1 row, but instead of adding a second C in the outer circle, wrap the strip around the 27mm stone and pass through the C on the other end of the strip to connect. Add the third C as usual. Pass through all 8 of the beads in the connecting unit again to tighten. Continue around to exit the outermost C in the new unit.

3 Flip your work over. Pick up 4B and pass through the first B again. Pass through the C in the adjacent unit and pass through the next B in the new unit. Pick up 1C and pass through the next B in the new unit. Pass through the next 5 outer beads in this unit plus 6 beads in the next 2 units, exiting the C on the spine.

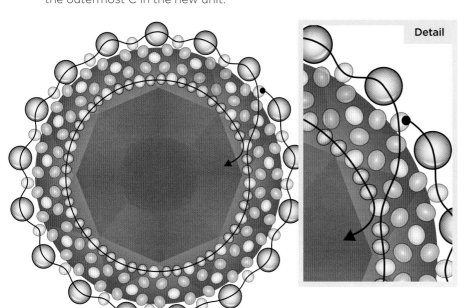

4 Pick up 1D and pass through the next C in the spine. Repeat to add pearls around the entire bezel. Pass down to the center of the bezel on the front of the pendant. Pick up 2A and pass through the next C. Repeat around the bezel. Pass through all of the beads in the round to tighten them.

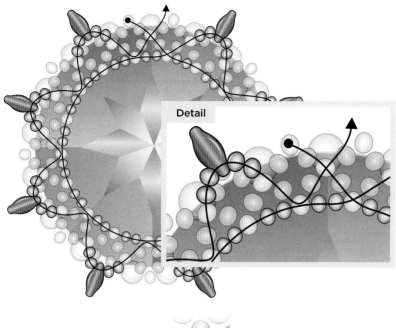

Detail

5 Weave to the back of the pendant and add 2A between each of the Cs in the center of the bezel as shown. Pass through 1B and 1C toward the spine. Pick up 2C, 1SD and 2C. Pass down through the C on the other side of the unit. Pass through the work to the C on the other side of the next unit and add another picot of 2C, 1SD, 2C. Repeat 6 more times around the pendant to add a total of 8 picots. Pass through 5 more beads to exit the B just before the spine of the bezel as shown.

— **TIP** —

Try to make the picots as tight as possible so the SuperDuos don't droop. Retracing the thread path at least once may also help.

6 To start the bail, pick up 1C and pass down through the B on the other side of the adjacent pearl. Pass under the next C to hide the thread and pass up through the B from the beginning of this step. Continue through the C just added. Working in right angle weave (see page 13), make a strip 12 units long.

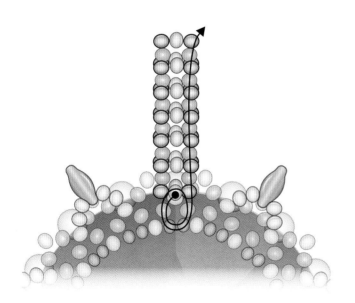

7 Fold the strip over and connect the last C to the bezel by passing through the B, 2A and B along the midline of the bezel. Continue through the C, B, 2A and B of the last unit again. Pick up 1C and pass through the next B in the bail. Continue adding C beads to the edge of the bail. When you get to the end of the first edge, pass around the first RAW unit from the previous step and continue adding C beads to the second edge of the bail.

8 Weave in your threads, tying a few half-hitch knots to secure. Trim the thread.

— **TIP** —

You may need to make your strip of RAW shorter or longer depending on the diameter of your rope. My bail is the perfect size for a Rosie Posie Rope *(page 48).*

Rosie Posie Rope

Once I had created my *Starflower* pendant (page 44), I needed something to hang it on. I tend to like three-sided ropes, whether tubular right angle weave, twisted herringbone or filled netting. I played around with tubular DDRAW, but I wanted to figure out a way to incorporate the SuperDuos and pearls to create a more cohesive color picture. As the piece evolved, I realized that the seed-bead sections could be made with netting instead of DDRAW. The end result is a much faster stitch with the same look and feel. Technically, this isn't a DDRAW piece anymore, but if you don't tell, I won't either!

MATERIALS

9 grams 11/0 Duracoat gold seed beads (A)

5 grams 11/0 matte metallic sage luster seed beads (B)

57 light cremerose glass pearls, 3mm

8 grams rose luster Super-Duo 2-hole beads (SD), 2.5mm × 5mm

1 gold magnetic clasp, 10mm

SIZE

Makes a necklace 18″ (46cm) long

This variation is made with just SuperDuos and seed beads.

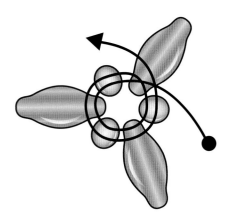

1 On a comfortable length of thread, string 1SD and 1A 3 times. Pass through all 6 beads and the first SD again. Pull snugly on both the ending and working threads to tighten.

Important

In this tutorial, the diagrams are drawn as if you are looking at the top of the tube, not the sides.

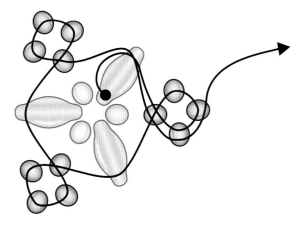

2 Pass through the second hole of the SD. *Pick up 4A and pass through the first A. Pass through the top hole of the next SD. Pull everything snug.* Repeat * to * twice. Pass through the first 3A you picked up in this step. You should now have a triangular tube.

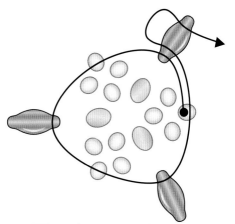

3 Pick up 1SD and pass through the up bead on the next picot. Repeat twice. Repeat the thread path of this step, if desired, to tighten. Pass through the next SD and the second hole of that SD.

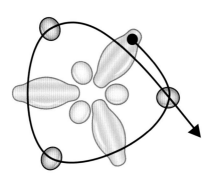

4 Pick up 1A and pass through the top hole of the next SD. Repeat twice. Pass through the first A and tighten.

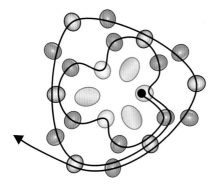

5 For netting row 1, pick up 1B, 1A and 1B. Skip the SD and pass through the next A. Repeat twice and then step up by going through the first B and A from this round.

For netting row 2, pick up 1B, 1A and 1B. Pass through the up A in the next net. Repeat twice and step up by going through the first B and A from this row.

Variation

To make the rope without the pearls, follow the instructions as written but skip steps 6 and 7. Add a third color to the mix by making the picots (step 2) with the third color. Use the first 2 colors for the rest of the steps.

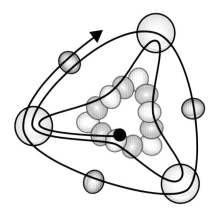

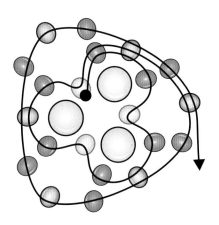

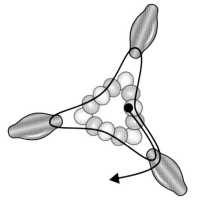

6 Pick up 1 pearl and pass through the next up bead in the round of netting just completed. Repeat twice. Pass through the first pearl again. Pick up 1A and pass through the next pearl. Repeat twice. Pass through the first A again.

7 Repeat step 5 to add another 2 rows of netting above the pearls.

8 Pick up 1SD and pass through the next up bead in the netting. Repeat twice. Pass through the next SD again.

9 Repeat steps 2–8 until the rope is the desired length. Pass through all of the beads in the last round again. String half of the clasp and secure it to a bead and SD that are opposite each other. Use multiple passes to secure. Weave in your threads, tying a few half-hitch knots, and trim. Repeat on the other side of the rope to attach the second half of the clasp.

Sundial

I recently discovered Lunasoft cabochons, and their beautiful glow just begged to be showcased. Starting with the bezel from *Starflower* (page 44), I modified the count to fit around the slightly smaller Lunasoft cab. The fit was a little more snug, so it required less embellishing to secure the cab. The DDRAW pattern is less pronounced in the bezel, so I made a simple DDRAW bail on which to hang the pendant. The rope on which my pendant hangs is a simple CRAW rope (page 14).

MATERIALS FOR
PENDANT ONLY

1 gram 15/0 Duracoat seafoam seed beads (A)

1 gram 11/0 Duracoat seafoam seed beads (B)

1 gram 11/0 Permanent Finish copper seed beads (C)

26 aqua vitrail SuperDuo 2-hole beads (SD), 2.5mm × 5mm

1 round mango Lunasoft cabochon, 18mm

1 round mango Lunasoft cabochon, 24mm

SIZE

Makes a pendant 1⅜" (4cm) wide and 3¼" (8cm) long

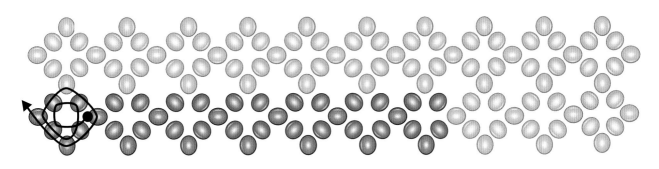

1 First, make a bezel for the 18mm cabochon. To do this, make a strip of DDRAW (see pages 22–23 for basic DDRAW instructions) 2 units wide and 10 units long with B beads in the inner pass and C beads in the outer pass.

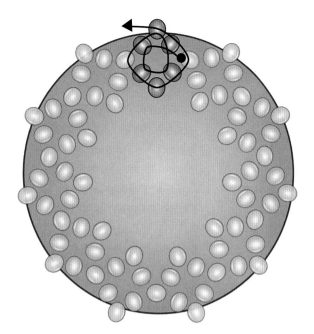

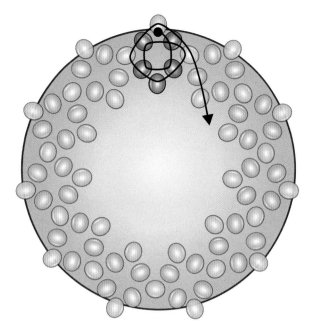

2 Add an eleventh unit to 1 row, but instead of adding a second C in the outer circle, wrap the strip around the 18mm cab and pass through the C on the other end of the strip to connect. Add the third C as usual. Pass through all 8 of the beads in the connecting unit to tighten them. Continue around the unit to exit the C on the outer edge.

3 Flip your work over. Pick up 4B and pass through the first B again. Pass through the C in the adjacent unit and pass through the next B in the new unit. Pick up 1C and pass through the next B in the new unit. Pass through the next 5 outer beads in this unit plus 2 beads in the next unit, exiting the C at the center of the circle.

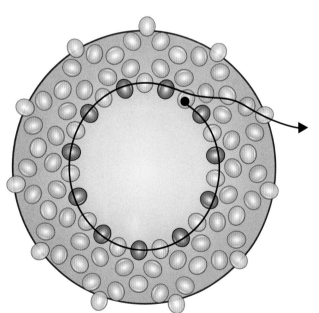

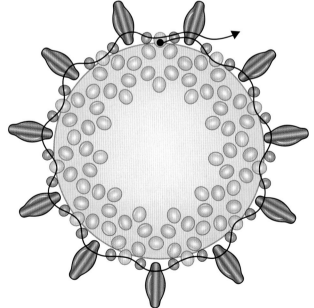

4 Pick up 1B and pass through the adjacent C in the next unit. Repeat around the rest of the circle. Repeat the thread path if necessary to tighten. Weave through the work to exit a connecting C between the front and back of the bezeled cab.

5 Pick up 1A, 1SD and 1A. Pass through the next C in the rim. Repeat around the circle. Repeat the thread path if necessary to tighten. Weave in the working and tail threads and trim. Set this component aside.

6 To make a bezel for the 24mm cabochon, follow steps 1–5. The initial strip will have 13 units and the connecting unit will be the fourteenth. Exit from an SD and pass through the second hole of that same SD.

7 Pick up 1B, 1SD and 1B. Pass through both holes of the next SD. Pass through the next A, C, A, both holes of the SD, the B and SD you just added. Pass through the second hole of the new SD. Pick up 1B and pass through the second hole of an SD in the first component. Pass through the first hole of the SD, 1A, 1C, 1A and both holes of the next SD. Pick up 1B and pass through the connecting SD. Repeat these thread paths as needed to secure. Weave in the working and tail threads, secure with half-hitch knots, and trim. Set these components aside.

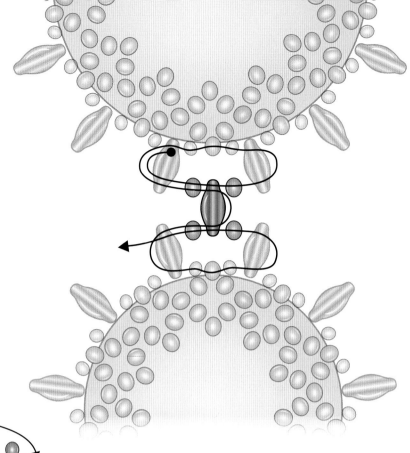

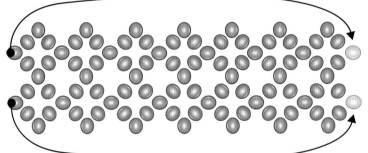

8 Create a strip of DDRAW 2 units wide and 5 to 9 units long. The number of units will depend on the diameter of the rope on which you wish to hang the pendant. An odd number of units is best. On the last unit, connect the ends of the strip by sharing the C from the first unit.

9 Weave through the work if necessary until you are exiting a C and headed toward the center of the strip as shown. Pick up 2A and pass through the C on the other side of the strip. Pick up the pendant and pass through an SD opposite where the 2 components are attached. Pass through the second hole of the SD, through the A, C and A on the pendant, through the 2 holes of the next SD and the C that you were exiting at the beginning of this step. Repeat the thread path a couple of times to secure. Weave in your threads, secure with half-hitch knots, and trim the threads.

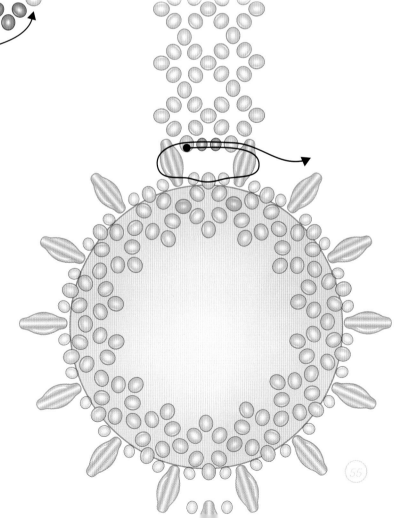

Chapter Two

Faux Right Angle Weave

As much as I love right angle weave, what I like least about it is how time-consuming it can be. All of the round and round and switching directions every unit made me want to find an easier way. Fortunately, I love problem solving with beads and puzzling out a solution to the problem was fun and challenging.

If you ask any beader what the primary rules of right angle weave are, they will probably answer the same way: stitch in right angles only and never move straight across from one unit to another. But what better way to explore new shapes and designs than by breaking the rules? When you step outside the box, new discoveries can be made.

Faux Right Angle Weave (FRAW) Primer

One of the most common things to do with a fabric of right angle weave is to embellish the spaces. There are two different spaces: the ones inside each unit and the ones in the corners between units. The spaces between units are the key to the secret of faux right angle weave. If you break the rule about not passing in a straight line from one unit to the next, another bead needs to fill in the space or thread will show. By filling this space as you build the base of right angle weave, you eliminate the need to switch directions with each unit. You still need to switch with subsequent rows, but it certainly cuts down on the time involved in the stitch.

FRAW has been around a while (I discovered the method while attempting to change bead sizes in a bracelet I was designing in 2010), and you may also see it called modified right angle weave (MRAW). I prefer to call it faux RAW, partly because I was already calling it this when I first heard the term MRAW, but also because when you stitch this way, you still have a piece that has the same basic structure as right angle weave. If you didn't know, you might not even be able to tell it was made differently. I generally use the term "modified" to describe a change in the underlying structure, such as the modified cubic right angle weave (CRAW) piece I made called *Toblerone* (in the gallery on page 137). Although the thread path in that piece is very similar to that of regular CRAW, the resulting piece has been modified to have only five sides to each unit instead of the usual six.

Use this method to make your FRAW strip as wide and as long as needed. Each row will change stitching directions. If you make a row and are stitching clockwise, the adjacent row will be stitched counterclockwise.

> ### — TIP —
>
> *If you are making a flat piece with multiple rows, it is best to use a smaller sized bead as a placeholder. Using the same size or larger bead as a placeholder works best in single row FRAW or if you are going to build another stitch off of the placeholders.*

MAKING THE FIRST ROW

1 On a comfortable length of thread, string 4A (11/0) beads for unit 1. Pass through the first A to make a square. Pass through all 4 beads again and pull snugly on the tail and working threads to tighten.

> ### — TIP —
>
> *Keep moderate tension while stitching. If you bead too tightly, the strip could curve or twist rather than lie flat.*

2 For unit 2 and subsequent units, pick up 1B (15/0) bead and 3A. Pass through the adjacent A from the previous unit and the first A just picked up. Repeat as desired. Take care not to go through the B placeholders more than once. Pass through the next 2 beads in the last unit.

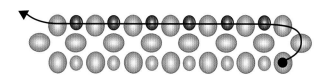

3 Pick up 1B and pass through the next A in the strip. Repeat down the length of the strip.

ADDING SUBSEQUENT ROWS

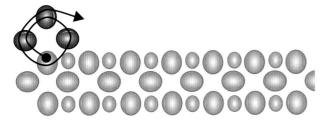 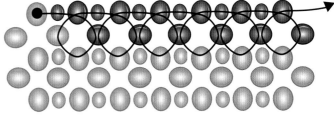

4 Pick up 3A and pass through the A being exited at the beginning of this step. Continue through the first 2A you picked up in this step.

5 Pick up 1B and 2A. Pass through the A from the adjacent unit in the previous row and the last A picked up in the previous unit. Pass through the first A picked up, taking care to skip the B just added. Make sure that the thread does not cross behind the B, or the work will twist. Repeat to complete the row.

6 Repeat steps 4 and 5 until the work is the desired size.

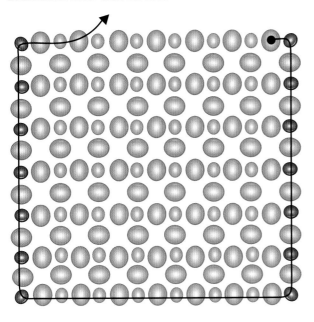

— TIP FOR LEFTIES —

The easiest way to work left-handed is to hold your work so that you are always stitching up and to the left. Rotate or flip the work with each new row. Once you get the stitch down, you will be able to apply the concept to other patterns.

EMBELLISHING THE EDGES

7 The edges of the FRAW strip will have empty spaces that are perfect for embellishing. You can add B beads between each A at this point or any other embellishment bead you desire, such as drops or magatamas. You can also easily add a row of peyote stitch to this open edge using the existing beads as up beads from which to build the peyote row.

Couplet

Two-hole beads are all the rage (and I happen to love them), so I am often trying to incorporate them into my designs. FRAW is an easy stitch to modify in order to add two-hole beads, whether they are SuperDuos, lentils, triangles, Tilas, bricks . . . the list is seemingly endless!

The easiest way to start working with a new stitch is to keep the basic thread path the same but change the beads or bead counts. Changing one bead size may mean changing the sizes or counts of the other beads, too. For example, using 8/0 beads for the main beads creates a space between units that a single 11/0 won't fill. Two 11/0 beads are too wide, but two 15/0 beads fit perfectly.

As I created my first row of *Couplet,* I played with the bead counts of my RAW circle as well as my placeholders. When I strung the lentils with just the 8/0 beads, I didn't like how much thread was showing, so I added a 15/0 bead to the inside circle. Doing that left less space between units, so my placeholders wound up being single 15/0 beads.

MATERIALS

2 grams 15/0 silver Permanent Finish seed beads (A)

1 gram 15/0 turquoise Permanent Finish seed beads (B)

2 grams 8/0 matte chocolate brown seed beads (C)

30 matte gold satin rounds, 4mm

60 opaque turquoise Picasso 2-hole lentils, 6mm

1 copper 2-hole slide clasp

SIZE

Makes a bracelet about 7" (18cm) long

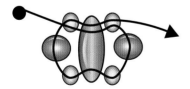

1 Start the first row by stringing 1A, a lentil, 1A, 1C and 1A. Pass through the second hole of the lentil. Pick up 1A, 1C and pass through the first 3 beads again. See pages 58–59 for basic FRAW instructions.

— TIP —

Work with loose to medium tension. If you work too tightly, the piece may buckle or curve.

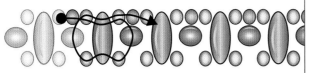 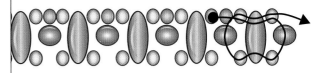

2 Pick up 1B, 1A, a lentil, 1A, 1C and 1A. Pass through the second hole of the lentil, pick up 1A and pass through the adjacent C. Pass through the A, lentil and A, skipping the B you picked up at the beginning of this step. Be careful not to cross your thread behind the B. Repeat this step until the strip is the desired length of the bracelet, minus the clasp.

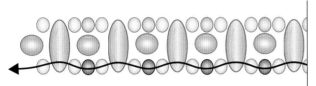 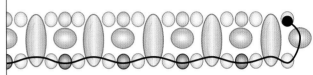

3 Continue through the next 4 beads around the end of the strip. Pick up 1B and pass through the next 3 beads. Add 1B between each set of A beads along the entire second edge. Watch your tension so that the piece lies flat.

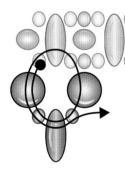

4 Exiting from the last A in the row, start the second row by picking up a 4mm round, 1A, a lentil, 1A and a 4mm round. Pass through the next-to-last A in the previous row and the next 6 beads as shown.

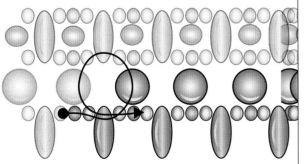 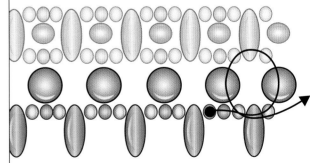

5 Pick up 1B, 1A, a lentil, 1A and a 4mm round. Pass through the A, lentil and A on the previous row. Pass through the adjacent 4mm round and through the next A, lentil and A, skipping the B. Take care not to cross the thread behind the B. Repeat this step down the length of the bracelet.

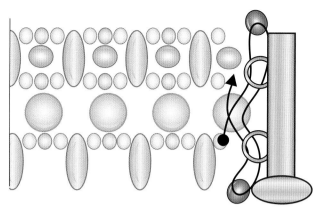

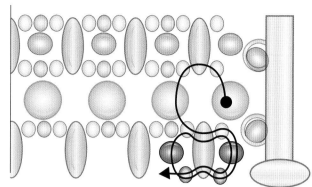

6 To add the first half of the clasp, pass through the final 4mm round. *Pass up through 1 hole of the slide clasp. Pick up 1C and pass down through the same hole of the clasp. Pass back through the 4mm round.* Repeat * to *. Repeat the entire thread path of this step once or twice to secure the clasp.

7 Weave through 3 beads on the first side of the bracelet as shown. Continue through the second 4mm round and then the next 3 beads to set up for the last row of seed beads. Pick up 1C and 1A. Pass through the second hole of the lentil. Pick up 1A and 1C. Pass through the adjacent A and the next 6 beads in the unit.

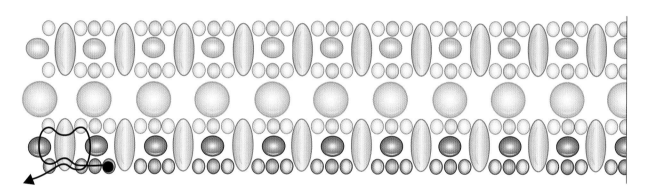

8 Pick up 1B and 1A. Pass through the second hole of the next lentil. Pick up 1A and 1C. Pass through the A next to the first hole of the lentil and through the next 6 beads in the unit, skipping the B. Repeat this step for the entire length of the bracelet.

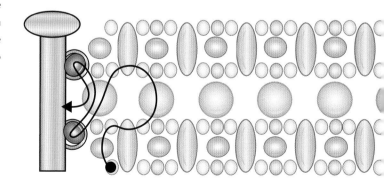

9 Continue through the next 4 beads of the last unit and then through the 4mm round and the next 3 beads in the central unit. Pass through the last 4mm round. Attach the second half of the clasp in the same manner you attached the first (step 6). Weave in your threads, tying a few half-hitch knots to secure. Trim the threads.

Fee Fi Faux Fun

One right angle weave technique that took me some time to learn is diagonal RAW. But once I had mastered making multiple rows of FRAW, I knew that I would be able to translate the stitch into a diagonal variation. My first version was done in just one color, but I soon realized that by using multiple colors I could draw the pattern out even more. Using multiple colors also made it easier to keep my place in the pattern. What developed is a playful, colorful bracelet that will grab the attention of anyone who sees it!

MATERIALS

1–3 grams each 15/0 seed beads in 3–7 colors (black will be designated AA, color 1 BB, color 2 CC, etc.)

1–2 grams each 11/0 seed beads in the same colors (black will be designated A, color 1 B, color 2 C, etc.)

6 gunmetal jump rings, 6mm

1 gunmetal 3-hole slide clasp

SIZE

Makes a bracelet about 7″ (18cm) long

— TIP —

One way to play around with patterns is to make a swatch using beads of the same color, preferably a light color bead with a matte finish. Then take a black-and-white photo of the piece, print it out, and use colored pencils or markers to pull out the patterns you see.

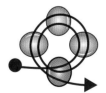

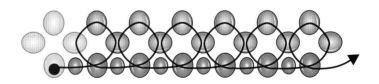

1 Using faux right angle weave, create 1 row of beads 7 units long. To start, string 1A and 3B. Pass through the A to make a square. Pass through all 4 beads again and pull snugly on the tail and working threads to tighten.

2 Pick up 1AA, 1A and 2B. Pass through the adjacent B and the A you just picked up. Repeat 5 more times. Take care not to go through the AA more than once.

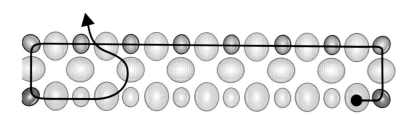

3 Pick up 1AA and pass through the next B. Pick up 1BB and pass through the next B. Continue in this manner, adding 1BB between each B, 7 more times until you get to the other end. Pick up 1AA and pass through the next A, AA and A. Pass through the adjacent B and then through the next B. Your thread should now be exiting the second B on that side and headed toward the short end of the row.

Using metallic colors in place of the bright colors transforms this playful bracelet into a more sophisticated variation.

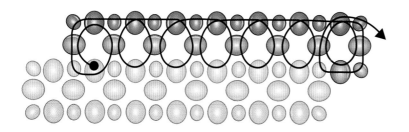

4 Create a second row of beads that is offset from the first row by 1 unit. To start, pick up 1B, 1A and 1B. Pass through the bead you are currently exiting, making a square. Pass through the adjacent BB and the first B you picked up in this step. Pick up 1AA and pass through the next A.

5 Pick up 1AA, 1A and 1B. Pass through the adjacent B from the first row to form a square, through the next B and through the A you just picked up. Repeat 4 more times.

6 Pick up 1AA, 1A and 2B. Pass through the adjacent B and the A you just picked up. Pick up 1AA, pass though the next B, pick up 1BB, pass through the next B, BB, B, A and AA.

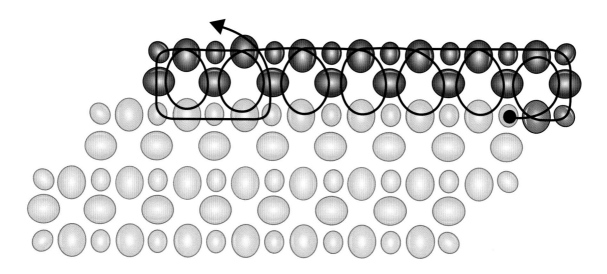

7 For row 3, pick up 1A and 3C. Pass through the first A again, forming a square. Pick up 1AA and pass through the next C. Pick up 1CC and pass through the next C. Pass through the C, AA, A and 2C again to tighten this unit, if you desire.

8 Pick up 1CC and 2C. Pass through the adjacent A, forming a square. Continue through the next 2C. Repeat 5 more times. Pick up 1CC, pass through the next C, AA, A, AA, A and 2C to exit the second-to-last C on the top row of beads as shown.

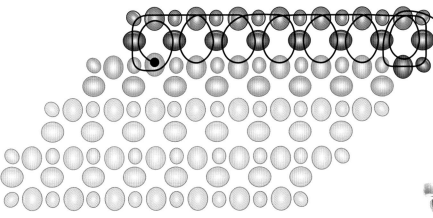

9 Pick up 1C, 1A and 1C. Pass through the bead you are currently exiting, making a square. Pass through the adjacent CC and the first C you picked up in this step. Pick up 1AA and pass through the next A.

10 Pick up 1AA, 1A and 1C. Pass through the adjacent C from the first row to form a square, through the next C, and through the A you just picked up. Repeat 4 more times.

11 Pick up 1AA, 1A and 2C. Pass through the adjacent C and the A you just picked up. Pick up 1AA, pass through the next C, pick up 1CC, pass through the next C, CC, C, A and AA.

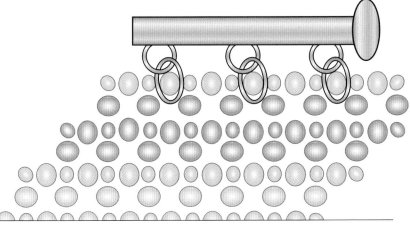

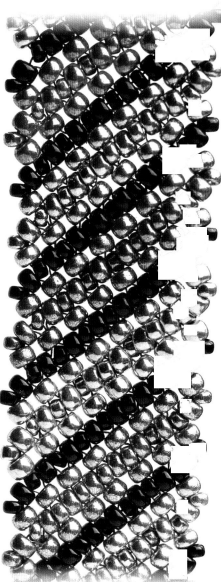

12 For all subsequent rows, repeat the instructions in steps 7–11, substituting the next color you are using in your bracelet. I used 6 colors in my original piece.

13 When the bracelet is the desired length minus the clasp, weave in your threads, tying a few half-hitch knots to secure them. Trim the threads. Attach the clasp to the second, fourth and sixth unit in the last row on each end using jump rings.

Firewheel Daisy

The first version of this fiery flower was made by setting a Lunasoft cabochon within a bezel and adding the two-hole daggers with FRAW to the back. Attaching the daggers was very difficult, though, so I set about creating the piece in reverse, starting with the daggers. I also wanted to add another stitch into the mix, so I made the neck straps with St. Petersburg stitch. FRAW plays a minor role in this piece, acting as a base from which the rest of the bezel is built.

MATERIALS

1 gram 15/0 gold Duracoat seed beads (A)

1 gram 15/0 berry Duracoat seed beads (AA)

5 grams 11/0 gold Duracoat seed beads (B)

3 grams 11/0 berry Duracoat seed beads (C)

36 astral pink bicones (D), 3mm

28 astral pink bicones (E), 4mm

1 volcano rivoli, 18mm

20 sunset maple 2-hole daggers

2 gold lobster clasps

1 gold jump ring

SIZE

Makes a choker about 13½" (34cm) long and a pendant 1½" (4cm) in diameter

1 On a long but comfortable length of thread, string 20 daggers through the second (middle) hole to start the petal base. Tie a knot and weave through a few of the daggers. Pass through the first hole of the dagger (now at the center of the circle). Pass through the first hole of all 20 daggers and then through 1 or 2 more.

2 To start the first round of the first layer, pick up 3B and pass through the dagger you are exiting, making a loop of seed beads over the dagger. Pass through the next dagger.

You can substitute an 18mm Lunasoft cabochon for the 18mm rivoli in this project

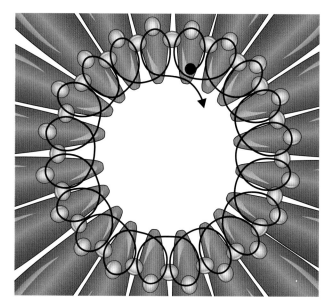

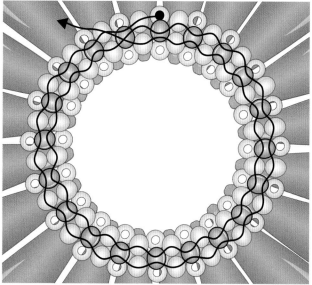

3 Pick up 2B and pass through the adjacent B from the previous unit. Pass through the dagger you were exiting at the beginning of this step. Pass through the next dagger.

4 Repeat step 3 until there are loops of seed beads over each of the 20 daggers in the base. On the final unit, you will need to pass up through the last B from the first unit (step 2) and pick up only 1B before passing down through the B from the previous unit. Pass through the dagger being exited.

5 For the second round of the first layer, pass through the other (second) hole of the dagger being exited. Repeat steps 2–4 to add another round of FRAW over the second holes of the daggers in the base.

6 To start the second layer, which is peyote stitch, weave up through 2B to exit a top bead in the first layer (round 2).

7 Pick up 1B and pass through the next top B in the round. Repeat all the way around the circle.

8 Step up by passing through the first B from the previous step. Zip up the layer by connecting the new round of beads to the top beads from the first layer (round 1). End this round by exiting a bead in the outside circle.

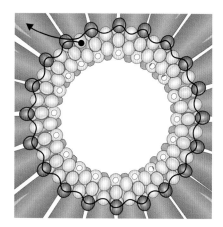

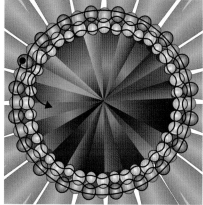

9 Pick up 1C and pass through the next B in the outer circle. Repeat 19 times. Pass through the first C again.

10 To start the peyote bezel, pick up 1C and pass through the next C in the circle from the previous step. Repeat around the bezel, adding beads between each C bead. Place the

rivoli in the bezel and then tighten the round. Step up by passing through the first C picked up in this step.

11 Add a round of peyote with B beads between each of the beads added in the previous step. Step up by passing through the first B picked up in this step.

12 Add a final round of peyote using A beads between each of the B from the previous step.

13 Weave in your threads, tying a few half-hitch knots to secure. Trim the threads.

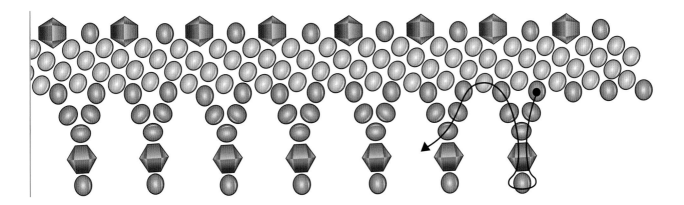

14 Use St. Petersburg stitch (see page 17) to make 2 single-row straps. Attach the clasp at the beginning of each as shown. On the turn edge, substitute a 3mm bicone for every other turn bead.

15 Attach the straps to the back of the pendant (as shown in the photo below). Stitch through the last row of beads in the strap and the hole of the dagger several times to secure. Do not trim threads yet.

16 On each strap, pass through the work to exit the fourth stop-stitch bead. Pick up 2C, 1E and 1AA. Pass back through the 4mm bicone and the next C. Pick up 1C and pass through the next stop-stitch bead. Pass through the next couple of beads to exit the next stop-stitch bead.

17 Repeat step 16 down the length of the strap, stopping a few units before the end of the strap. Weave in your threads, secure with half-hitch knots, and trim the threads.

— TIP —

To make a convertible choker or necklace, make a strap of double St. Petersburg with lobster clasps at each end. Attach this double strap to the existing piece with jump rings.

The reverse side of the *Firewheel Daisy* pendant

Firewheel Spinner

The original *Firewheel Daisy* pendant that I mentioned in the previous project was made with a St. Petersburg bezel. I wasn't able to incorporate the stitch in the revised pendant, but it got me thinking. I decided I wanted a more elaborate embellishment for the petal base, with the St. Petersburg flaring out and swirling around the bezel. The peyote stitch layer provides an easy place turn to around, and the layer can be made to swirl in either direction. In the steps that follow, I include instructions for spiraling in both a clockwise and counterclockwise direction.

MATERIALS

1 gram 15/0 gold Duracoat seed beads (A)

2 grams 11/0 gold Duracoat seed beads (B)

3 grams 11/0 berry Duracoat seed beads (C)

20 ultra luster green Super-Duo 2-hole beads, 2.5mm × 5mm (SD)

1 pearl white Lunasoft cabochon, 18mm

20 sunset maple 2-hole daggers

2 gold jump rings, 6mm

1 gold ball chain with clasp

SIZE

Makes a pendant about 1½" (4cm) in diameter

You can substitute an 18mm rivoli for the 18mm Lunasoft cabochon in this project.

1 Follow steps 1–9 of *Firewheel Daisy* (pages 69–70) to create the base.

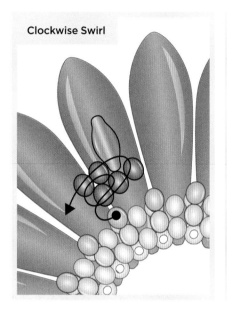

Clockwise Swirl

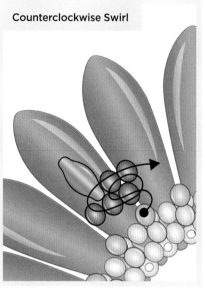

Counterclockwise Swirl

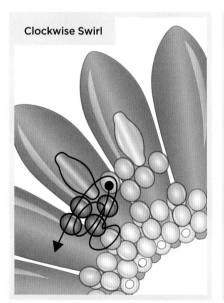

Clockwise Swirl

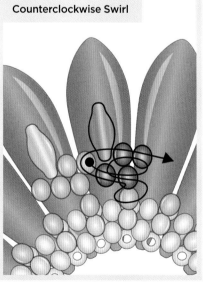

Counterclockwise Swirl

2 Make the second petal layer using the St. Petersburg stitch. Pick up 4C and pass through the first 2C. Pick up 1C and 1SD. Pass through the second 2C of the first 4 picked up in this unit. (Follow the Clockwise Swirl diagrams to stitch in a counterclockwise direction to acheive a clockwise swirl. Or follow the Counterclockwise Swirl diagrams to stitch in a clockwise direction to achieve a counterclockwise swirl.)

3 Pick up 4C and pass through the first 2C. Pass through the next C from the last round added in step 1. This is an anchor bead. Pass back through 3C. Pick up 1SD. Pass through the second 2C of the first 4 you picked up in this step.

4 Repeat step 3 seventeen times.

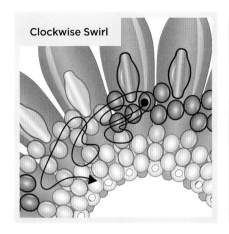

Clockwise Swirl

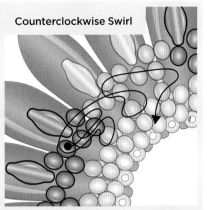

Counterclockwise Swirl

5 Pick up 2C and pass through the third C from step 2. Pick up 1C and pass through the first 2C you picked up in this step. Pass through the next anchor bead and back through the 3C. Pick up 1SD and pass through the next 4C. Pass through the last anchor bead and back through the next 2C. Pass through the next 4C and the next anchor bead.

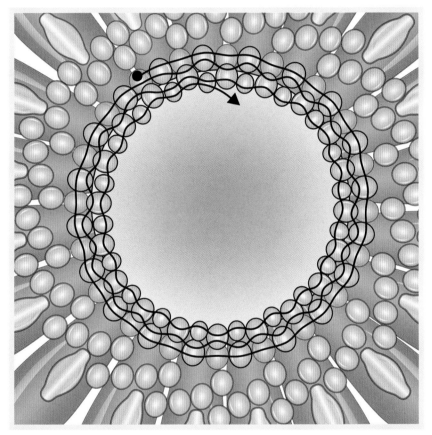

6 For the final layer, work in peyote stitch. Pick up 1B and pass through the next anchor bead in the circle (clockwise or counterclockwise, depending on which way your thread is exiting the anchor bead). Repeat around the circle, adding beads between each anchor bead. Place the cabochon in the bezel and then tighten the round. Step up by passing through the first B you picked up in this step.

7 Add a round of peyote with B beads between each of the beads added in the previous step. Step up by passing through the first B you picked up in this step.

8 Add a final round of peyote using A beads between each of the Bs from the previous step.

9 To finish, weave in your working thread, tying a few half-hitch knots to secure. Trim the threads.

10 Put a needle on your tail thread and weave through 2 or 3 daggers. Pick up a jump ring and pass back through a dagger. Stitch through the jump ring and through the dagger again. Repeat several times to secure the jump ring. Attach another jump ring to string a chain. Weave in your thread, tie a half-hitch know to secure, and trim the thread.

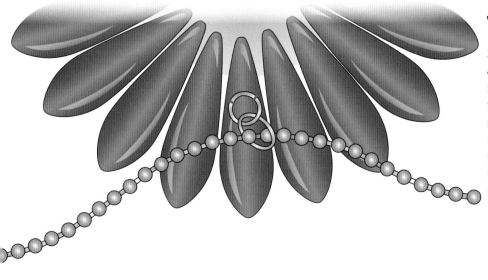

Off the Cuff

Cubic right angle weave (CRAW) (page 12) is very popular, and I love it. Every time I look, it seems that a new variation of it has been discovered. Having done a fair amount of CRAW myself, I know that adding multiple rows is time-consuming and difficult, more so when using different types or sizes of beads. I decided to take a base layer of FRAW and see if I could expand it to a cubic version without making it complicated. I discovered that I could indeed make a dimensional piece quite easily. Plus, by using the elongated fire-polished beads on the top layer and 8/0 seed beads in the base, the finished piece has a natural and comfortable curve.

MATERIALS

4 grams 11/0 silver Permanent Finish seed beads (A)

12 grams 8/0 gilt-lined smoky opal alabaster seed beads (B)

234 metallic teal fire-polished beads (C), 4mm

1 silver 2-hole slider clasp

SIZE

Makes a bracelet about 6¾" (17cm) long and ⅞" (2cm) wide

1 For the base, make a strip of FRAW (see pages 58–59 for basic FRAW instructions) that's 3 units long. Use B (8/0) beads for the rounds and A (11/0) beads for the placeholders. Continue adding rows until the strip is the necessary length for the finished cuff. Every 5 rows will make around 1" (3cm) of finished work. Flip the work over between rows, if it is more comfortable.

— **TIP** —

To make a wider cuff, you can add units to your base. The wider the base, the more the cuff will curve, so a longer base (and more fire-polished beads) will be required.

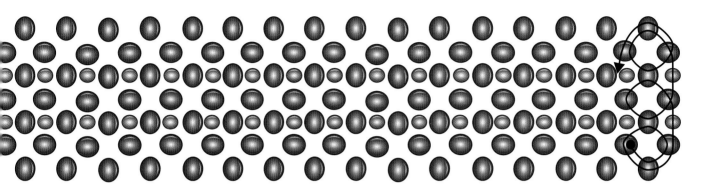

2 Weave around the last unit to exit the shared B between the last 2 rows. You will be headed toward the center of the work.

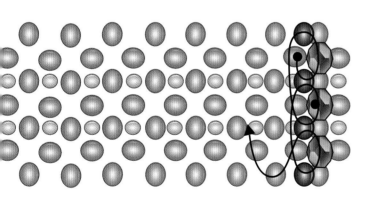

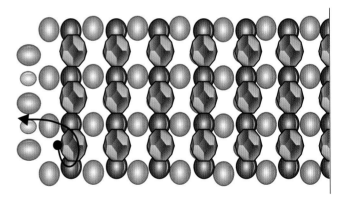

3 For part 1 of the top layer, work in FRAW to add vertical rows to the length of the base. Pick up 1B, 1C and 1B. Pass through the B that you are exiting.

4 Pass through the next A and B in the base. Pick up 1B and 1C. Pass down through the adjacent B (the first one picked up in the previous step) and then pass through the B that you passed through at the beginning of this step, skipping the A. Repeat this step for the last unit in the row.

5 Pass through the next 2B in the base.

6 Repeat the previous 3 steps to add vertical rows down the length of the base. Do not add a vertical row to the very last line of the strip. Do not pass through the next 2B in the base after adding the last row; instead, pass up through the B and C in the last unit you added.

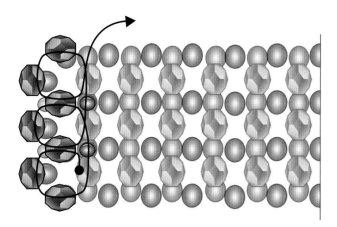

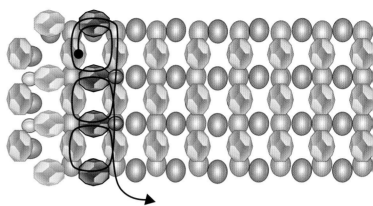

7 Complete the top layer by connecting the vertical rows. As you work, the rows will spread out and the cuff will start to curve. Pick up 3C and pass through the C you are exiting.

8 Pick up 1A and pass through the next C. Pick up 2C and pass through the first C from the last step. Repeat this step once.

9 Pick up 1C and pass through the adjacent C in the next vertical row. Pick up 1C and pass through the C you were exiting at the beginning of this step. Pass through the next 2C in this new unit. Pick up 1A and pass through the next C in the vertical row. Pick up 1C and pass through the adjacent C in the previous vertical row. Pass through the next 2C in the new unit. Pick up 1A and pass through the next C in the vertical row. Pick up 1C and pass through the adjacent C in the previous vertical row. Pass through the next 2C in the new unit.

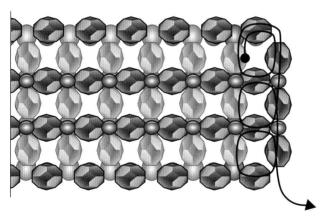

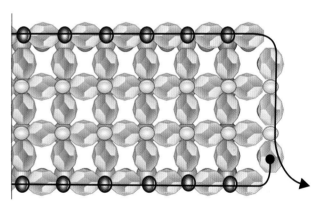

10 Repeat the previous step down the length of the cuff. After exiting the third C in the last vertical row, pick up 3C and pass through the bead you are currently exiting. Pass through the next 2C. Pick up 1A and 2C. Pass through the middle C from the last vertical row and the next 2C in the unit. Pick up 1A and 2C. Pass through the last C in the vertical row and the next 2C in the unit.

11 To finish the top layer, pass through the next C in the top layer. Continue adding 1A between each edge C of the top layer until you are exiting the C you were exiting at the beginning of this step. The last 2A will already be in place, so do not add any A beads on that edge.

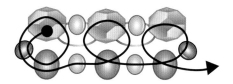

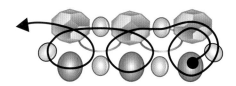

12 For the first half of the clasp, pick up 1A and pass through the first B in the base. Pick up half of the clasp and place it between the top and bottom layers. Pass up through the nearest clasp loop and pass through the first C. Pass through the next 4 beads. Pass up through the next clasp loop and pass through the middle C. Pass down through the first clasp loop and through the middle B in the base and the next 2 beads. Pick up 1A and pass through the last C in the top row. Pass down through the second loop and through the last B in the base.

13 Pass through the beads of the last units again to secure the clasp. Follow the thread path in the diagram. Weave in your thread, tying a few half-hitch knots to secure. Trim the thread.

— TIP —

Note that the first four illustrations on this page show the side view of adding the clasp.

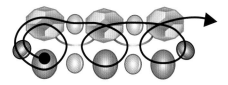

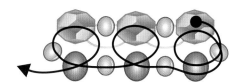

14 At the tail end, use the tail thread to pick up 1A and pass through the first C in the top row. Place the other side of the clasp between the top and bottom layers and pass down through the nearest clasp loop. Pass through the B, A and C of the first unit again. Pass through 1A and the middle C. Pass down through the second clasp loop and through the middle B. Pass up through the first clasp loop and through the middle C again. Pass through 1A and the last C in the row. Pick up 1A and pass through the last B in the bottom row. Pass up through the second clasp loop and through the C of the last unit.

15 Pass through the beads of the new units again to secure the clasp. Follow the thread path as shown in the diagram. Weave in your thread, tying a few half-hitch knots to secure. Trim the thread.

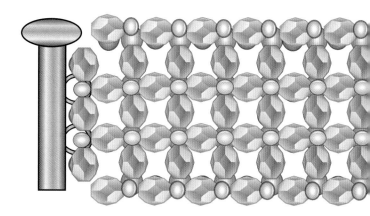

Top view after the whole bracelet is complete.

The bronze version is made with 4 FRAW units in each row and skips step 11 where 11/0 beads were added along the outside edge.

— TIP —

If your 11/0 beads have dropped down below the fire-polished beads, try popping them up with your needle to bring them back to the top.

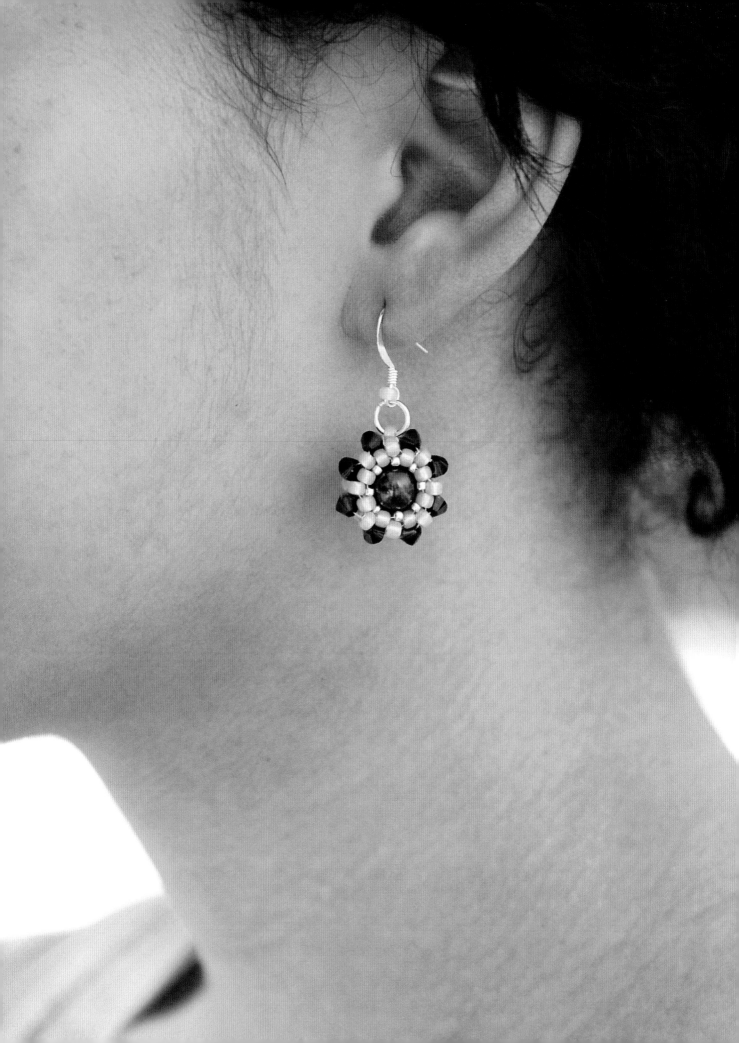

Wheelies

RAW is a great stitch for bezels and using FRAW makes it even easier. Seed beads and glass pearls make an elegant and classic pair of earrings. The larger holes of the 8/0 beads allow them to fit over the ear-wire loop, making for an even more custom look.

MATERIALS

1 gram 15/0 silver Permanent Finish seed beads (A)

2 grams 8/0 gilt-lined smoky opal alabaster seed beads (B)

16 purple velvet bicone crystals (C), 4mm

2 dark purple glass pearls, 8mm

2 silver jump rings, 6mm, 22- or 24-gauge

2 silver ear wires

1 Make a strip of FRAW (see pages 58–59 for basic FRAW instructions) that's 7 units long. Use B (8/0) beads for the rounds and A (15/0) beads for the placeholders.

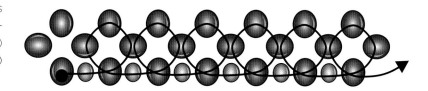

2 To connect the ring, pick up 1A and 1B. Pass through the B on the end of the starting edge. Pick up 1B and pass through the B on the end of the working edge. Pass through the first B you picked up.

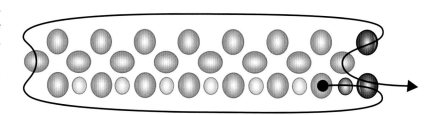

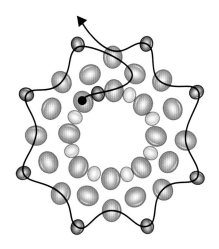

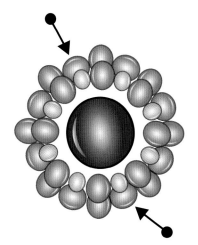

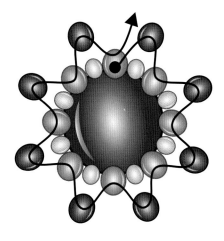

3 Pick up 1A and pass through the next 3B of the next unit. Pick up 1A and pass through the next B. Repeat around the circle, adding 1A between each edge B.

4 Add a pearl to the center and use peyote stitch for spokes. To start, pass through the next B in the current unit; this is the first anchor bead. This should be a center B, not an edge B. Pass down through the middle of the unit, pick up a pearl, and pass through the B exactly opposite the center B being exited; this is the second anchor bead. Pass back through the pearl (be careful not to catch the thread between beads in the strip when turning around) and pass through the first anchor bead again. The anchor beads are marked in the diagram.

5 Pass through the next edge B. Pick up 1B and pass through the next edge B in the bezel. Repeat around the circle.

6 Weave to the second side of the bezel and repeat the last step to add spokes all the way around.

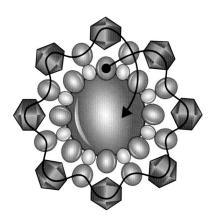

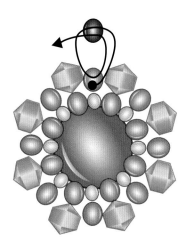

7 To finish, step up to exit one of the spoke beads just added. Pick up 1C and pass through the next spoke bead on the opposite side of the bezel. Repeat around the circle. The crystals will zigzag around the bezel.

8 After adding the final crystal and passing through the last spoke B, pick up 1B and pass through the spoke B and the new B, laddering them together, top to bottom. Pass through the opposite spoke B and the new B again, laddering them together as well. The new B will sit between the front and back sides of the piece.

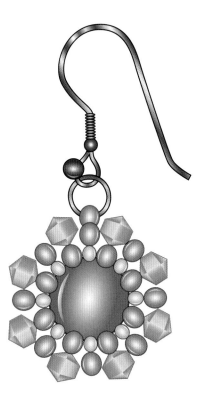

— **TIP** —

If too much thread is showing on either side of your crystals, pick up a 15/0 seed bead before and after picking up the crystal.

9 Pass a jump ring through the last B added. If it doesn't fit, add a loop of 15/0 seeds instead of the jump ring. Weave in your threads and tie a few half-hitch knots to secure. Trim the thread. Put 1B on the loop of the ear wire and then attach to the jump ring (or loop of seeds). Repeat to make the second earring.

Shoulder Dusters

I love teeny tiny seed beads. The smaller the better. And I love long dangly earrings. With just a few slight changes to *Wheelies* (page 82), the look changes dramatically. Use threader-style ear wires to make it easy to change the length of the earring from chin length to super long.

MATERIALS

1 gram 11/0 silver Permanent Finish seed beads (A)

22 jet AB2X velvet bicone crystals (B), 3mm

2 iridescent green Swarovski pearls, 8mm

2 silver thread guards

2 silver threader ear wires

— TIP —

If threaders bother your ears or you don't have any threaders on hand, use a long piece of silver chain instead. Attach the chains to silver ear wires.

These earrings work up quickly with few materials. Change up the colors to have a pair to match everything in your wardrobe!

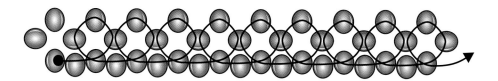

1 Make a strip of FRAW (see pages 58–59 for basic FRAW instructions) that's 10 units long. Use A (11/0) beads for both the rounds and the placeholders.

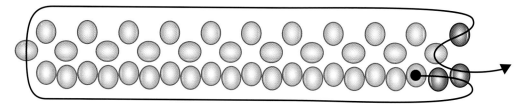

2 To connect the ring, pick up 2A. Pass through the A on the end of the starting edge. Pick up 1A and pass through the A on the end of the working edge. Pass through the second A you picked up.

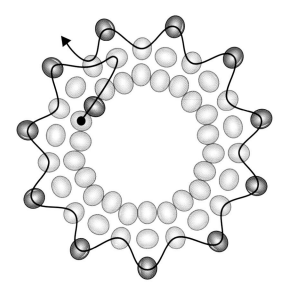

3 Pick up 1A and pass through the next 3A of the next unit. Pick up 1A and pass through the next edge A. Repeat around the circle, adding 1A between each edge A.

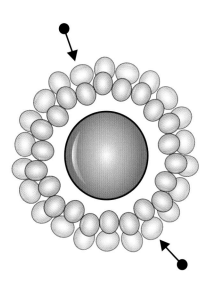

4 Add a pearl to the center and use peyote stitch to create spokes. To start, pass through the next A in the current unit; this is the first anchor bead and should be a center A, not an edge A. Pass down through the middle of the unit, pick up a pearl and pass through an A opposite the center A being exited; this is the second anchor bead. Pass back through the pearl (be careful you don't catch the thread between beads in the strip when turning around) and through the first anchor bead again. The anchor beads are marked in the diagram.

— TIP —

Not all beads are exactly the same size. When making your strip, before joining the ends together, check the size around your 8mm pearl. The strip's ends should not quite meet before you add the last connecting unit. You may need to delete or add a unit in order for the bezel to fit.

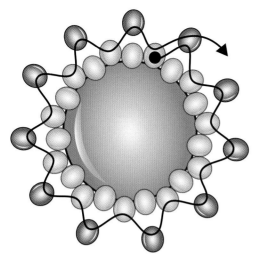

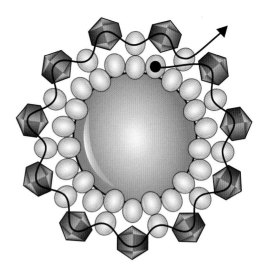

5 Pass through the next edge A. Pick up 1A and pass through the next edge A in the bezel. Repeat around the circle.

6 Weave to the second side of the bezel and repeat the last step to add spokes all the way around.

7 Step up to exit one of the spoke beads just added. Pick up 1B and pass through the next spoke bead on the same side of the bezel. After adding all of the crystals, pass through them again, but this time attach them to the spoke beads on the other side of the bezel.

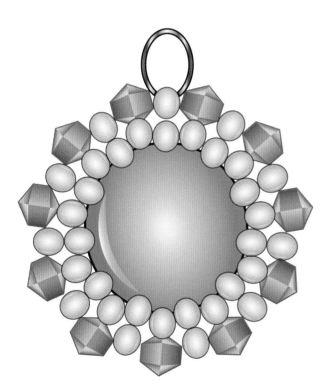

8 After passing through the final crystal and the last spoke A, pick up a thread guard. Pass through the spoke A on the other side of the bezel and back through the thread guard. Pass through the other side of the spoke A on the first side. Repeat, if desired, to secure the thread guard. Attach your threader to the guard. Repeat to make the second earring.

— TIP —

If the threaders do not have open rings, add one when attaching the thread guard. Otherwise, attach the threader and thread guard together with jump rings.

Yo-Yo Reversible Pendant

I wanted to continue with the idea of FRAW as a bezel base, so I pulled out some 18mm Lunasoft cabochons and played with the bead counts until the bezel fit perfectly. And because Lunasoft cabs have a flat back, two cabs in different colors can be placed back to back. Progressively smaller seed beads work quite well as placeholder beads in the initial FRAW circle and then in cinching the bezel around the cabs.

MATERIALS

1 gram 15/0 silver Permanent Finish seed beads (A)

1 gram 11/0 gilt-lined seafoam seed beads (B) (572)

1 gram 11/0 gilt-lined dark lavender seed beads (C) (574A)

1 gram 8/0 silver Permanent Finish seed beads (D)

18 emerald AB2X bicone crystals (E), 3mm

18 siam AB2X bicone crystals (F), 3mm

1 grape Lunasoft cabochon, 18mm

1 spearmint Lunasoft cabochon, 18mm

1 silver thread guard

18″ (46cm) silver snake chain with clasp

SIZE

Makes a pendant about 1⅛″ (3cm) in diameter

The reverse side of the pendant

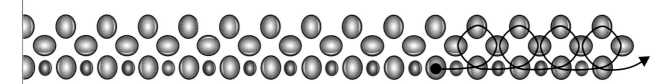

1 Make a strip of FRAW (see pages 58–59 for basic FRAW instructions) that's 17 units long. Use D (8/0) beads for the rounds and B (11/0) beads for the placeholders.

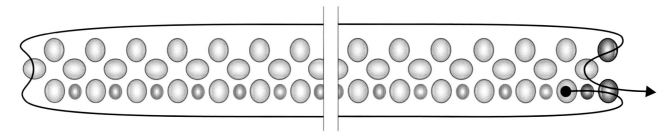

2 To connect the ring, pick up 1B and 1D. Pass through the D on the end of the starting edge. Pick up 1D and pass through the D on the end of the working edge. Pass through the first D you picked up.

— TIP —

Caution: If the chain won't fit through the thread guard, you will need to string it onto the thread guard in step 9.

Side view

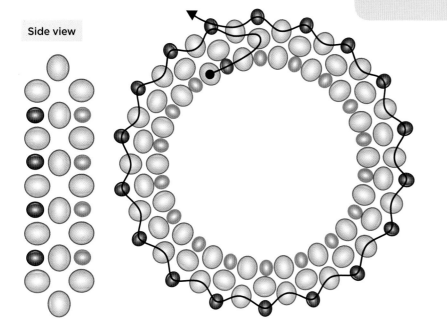

3 Pick up 1B and pass through the next 3D of the next unit. Pick up 1C and pass through the next edge D. Repeat around the circle, adding 1C between each edge D. Pass through the first C added.

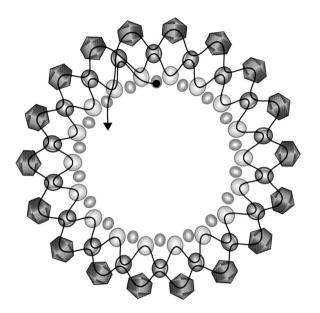

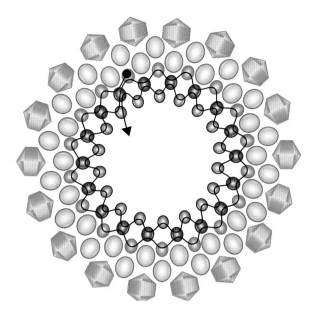

4 Pass through the next D. Pick up 1D and pass through the next D on the edge of the ring. Repeat 17 times. Pass through the first D you added in this round. This round will sit perpendicular to the base ring.

5 Pick up 1F and pass through the next D in the round just added. Repeat 17 times. Pass through the next D in the original ring, then pass through the next C.

6 For side 1 of the inner rounds, pick up 1C and pass through the next C. Repeat 17 times. Pass through the first C you added.

7 Pick up 1A and pass through the next C in the previous round. Repeat 17 times.

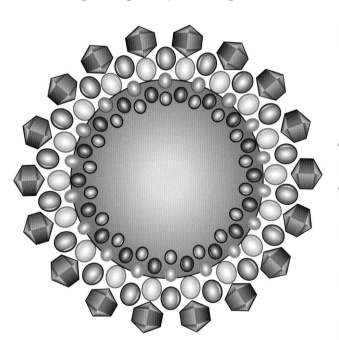

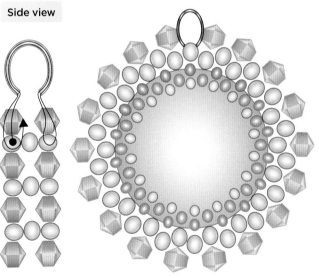

Side view

8 To start side 2, weave to the other side of the work. Repeat steps 4–5 for the outer rounds, substituting E for F and B for C. Insert both Lunasoft cabs and repeat steps 6–7, substituting B for C, to complete the bezel.

9 To finish, weave to a D next to one of the outer crystals. Pick up a thread guard. Pass through the D on the opposite side of the pendant and back through the thread guard. Pass through the other side of the D on the first side. Repeat, if desired, to secure the thread guard. Weave in your threads and trim.

10 String the snake chain through the thread guard.

Chapter Three

Layered Right Angle Weave

If you are anything like me, once you start using FRAW instead of traditional RAW, you'll want to use it all the time. It can be pretty quick to work up a strip of FRAW that can then be used as the base of a more elaborate or structural piece. One day while I was experimenting with FRAW, I made a long length with 8/0 seed beads. I manipulated the piece by twisting and curving it, noticing that if the rows were placed next to each other, but offset slightly, they nestled together nicely. I really liked the look, so the next time I made a strip of FRAW, I connected the placeholder beads as well, essentially making a second layer of FRAW offset from the base. I call this resulting stitch layered right angle weave (LRAW).

Layered Right Angle Weave (LRAW) Primer

LRAW is strong and structural, like cubic right angle weave (page 14), but it is more flexible (at least from front to back; it isn't as flexible from side to side). It is simpler than CRAW and a little bit faster to do as well. I love the snakelike feel of LRAW made with just 11/0 beads, especially in one long meandering double-sided rope. To make the piece reversible, just use a different color bead for the middle of each layer and the same color on both edges.

MATERIALS

5–6 grams 11/0 Permanent Finish steel seed beads (A)

3 grams 11/0 frosted amethyst berry seed beads (B)

3 grams 11/0 matte metallic sage luster seed beads (C)

2 silver thread guards

2 silver jump rings, 5mm or 6mm

1 silver trailer-hitch clasp

SIZE

Makes a rope about 34" (86cm) long

IT'S A WRAP NECKLACE / BRACELET

1 On a comfortable length of thread, string 4 beads in this order: ABAB. Pass through the first A to make a square. Leave a 6" (15cm) tail. Pass through all 4 beads again and pull snugly on the tail and working threads to tighten. This is unit 1 of the base row.

— TIP —

Adding the second layer will shorten the strip. It may be useful to leave a longer tail that can be used to lengthen the rope if necessary.

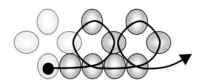

2 For all subsequent units in the base, pick up 2A, 1B and 1A. Pass through the adjacent B and the second A you picked up. Take care not to go through the first A (the placeholder) you picked up more than once.

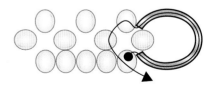

3 Once the strip is the desired length, pick up a thread guard and pass through the A on the other side of the final unit. Continue through the next 2 beads of the last unit. Repeat the thread path at least once.

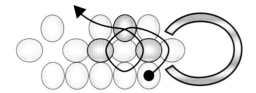
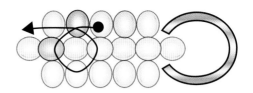

4 Make the second layer, which is FRAW offset from the first layer. Pass through the next 2 beads of the last unit of the base. Pick up 1A and 1C. Pass through the last placeholder A on the first side. Pick up 1C. Pass through the first A you picked up in this step and the second A on the second side. This is unit 1 of the top row.

5 For all subsequent units in the top row, pick up 1A and 1C. Pass through the opposite placeholder on the first side and through the C from the previous unit. Pass through the A you picked up and the next A on the second side.

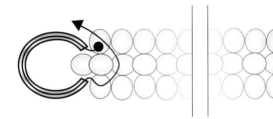

6 After adding the final unit on the top layer, pick up another thread guard and pass through the A on the opposite side. Pass through the next 2 beads of the end unit on the base. Repeat this thread path at least once.

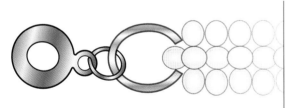
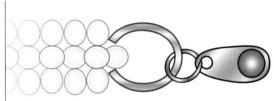

7 Weave in your working and tail threads, tie a few half-hitch knots, and trim. Attach the clasp to each end by connecting jump rings to the thread guards and the clasp loops.

— TIP —

To make a strip with different colors on each side (see Faux Ribbon Pendant *on page 114,* Circle Gets the Square *on page 118, and* Kiss Me Quick *on page 124), make the base row with one color for the units and the second color as placeholders. When adding beads to the second layer, pick up only beads the same color as the placeholders from the first layer of the strip.*

Reversible Braided Bracelet

One of the things I love about this layered technique is that while the resulting rope is sturdy like CRAW (page 14), it is not as substantial. The relative flatness of the rope works well in this reversible braided bracelet.

MATERIALS

7 grams 11/0 Permanent Finish silver seed beads (A)

2 grams 11/0 gilt-lined seafoam seed beads (B)

2 grams 11/0 gilt-lined dark lavender seed beads (C)

6 silver jump rings, 5mm or 6mm

1 silver 3-strand slide clasp

6 silver thread guards (optional)

SIZE

Makes a bracelet about 7" (18cm) long

— TIP —

Each finished rope in the sample is 7" (18cm) long, which shrinks to 6½" (17cm) when braided (not including the clasp).

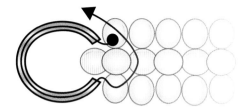 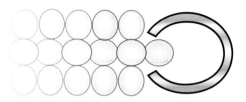

1 Make a rope of LRAW (see pages 96–97 for basic LRAW instructions) the desired length. Add thread guards to each end of the strip if desired. Use A (11/0) beads for the edges, and B and C (11/0) beads for the spines.

2 Weave in your working and tail threads and trim them. Make 2 more ropes the same length as the first. Attach the clasp to the first end by connecting jump rings to the thread guards and the clasp loops. If you aren't using thread guards, attach the jump ring directly to the last unit on the base of each rope.

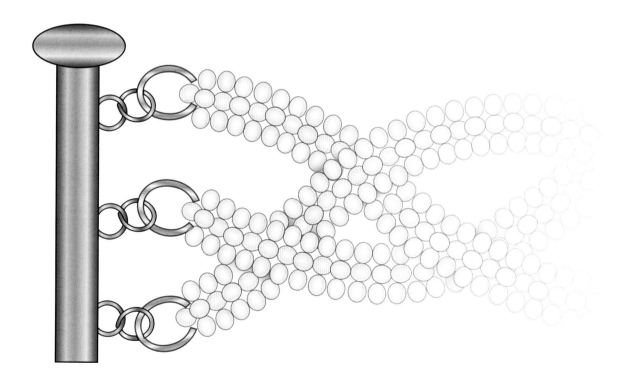

3 While the first half of the clasp is attached to each rope, braid the ropes together and attach them to the second half of the clasp. Cross the left rope over the middle and then the right over the middle (which started out as the left). Continue in this manner. The tighter the braid, the shorter the bracelet will be, so measure carefully before attaching the second half of the clasp.

This bracelet is soft and slinky to wear.

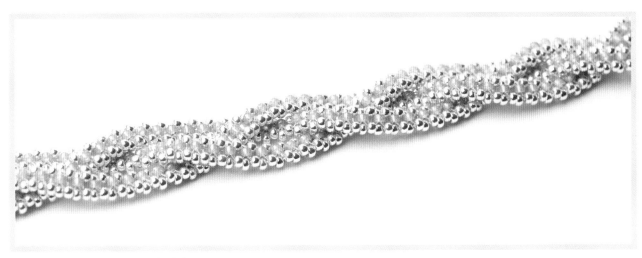

The reverse side of the bracelet is just as gorgeous.

Crystal Inclusion Reversible Bracelet

When I made my *Yo-Yo Reversible Pendant* (page 90), I initially planned to hang it on LRAW ropes. I tried several variations, none of which I ended up liking. Instead of taking the ropes apart or putting them in my box of unfinished pieces, however, I decided to use them to create an entirely new piece.

MATERIALS

5 grams 11/0 Permanent Finish silver seed beads (A)

2 grams 11/0 gilt-lined dark lavender seed beads (B)

2 grams 11/0 gilt-lined seafoam seed beads (C)

1 gram 15/0 Permanent Finish silver seed beads (D)

30 siam AB2X bicone crystals (E), 3mm

29 emerald AB2X bicone crystals (F), 3mm

4 silver jump rings, 5mm or 6mm

1 silver 2-strand slide clasp

SIZE

Makes a bracelet about 6¾″ (17cm) long

— TIP —

Work with loose to medium tension. Adding the second layer as well as stitching the strips together will tighten and shorten the pieces a little bit.

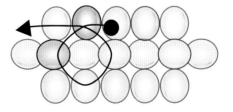

1 Make a rope of LRAW the desired length (see pages 96–97 for basic LRAW instructions). Use A (11/0) beads for the edges, B (11/0) beads for the spine of the base layer, and C (11/0) beads for the spine of the top layer. The number of units in the base should be odd. My sample bracelet has 51 units in the base.

2 After adding the final unit on the top layer, set the strip aside. Repeat step 1 to create another strip of the same length. Make sure the number of units in the 2 strips are identical.

3 In the following steps, you'll be connecting the 2 strips. Before doing that, count the number of units in each. Take the total number of units on the base (which will be 1 unit longer than the top layer), subtract 29, and then divide by 2. The resulting number is how many Bs you need to use in the next section before switching to bicones.

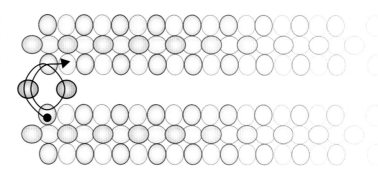

4 Place the strips next to each other, with the working thread between them and the color B beads on top. Pick up 1B and pass through the last A on the second strip. Pick up 1B and pass through the last A on the first strip (the bead you were exiting at the beginning of this step). Pass through the next 2 beads in the new unit. This is unit 1.

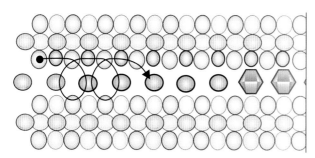

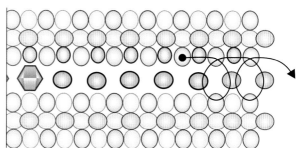

5 For all subsequent units, pick up 1D and pass through the next A in the strip. Pick up 1B and pass through the adjacent A from the other strip and the last B from the previous unit. Pass through the A from the first strip. Repeat this step until you have used the number of Bs from your previous calculation. At this point, substitute E for B until all 30 crystals are used, then switch back to B.

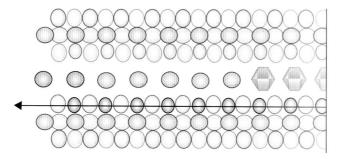

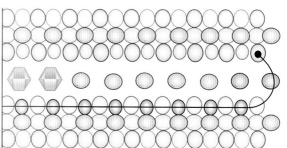

6 Pass through the next 2 beads of the last connecting unit. Pick up 1D and pass through the next A in the strip. Repeat down the length of the strip.

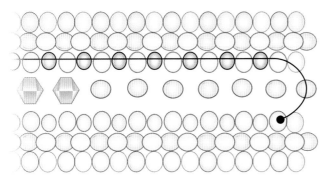

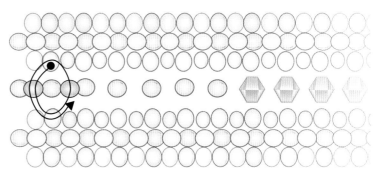

7 Flip your work over so that the color C beads are on top. Pass through the next 2 beads in the last connecting unit plus the next A in the row. Pick up 1D and pass through the next A in the strip. Repeat down the length of the strip. Make sure to go through only one A bead after adding the last D.

8 Pick up 1C and pass through the opposite A. Pick up 1C and pass through the A being exited at the beginning of this step. Pass through the next 2 beads in this new unit. This is unit 1.

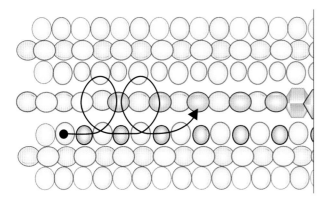

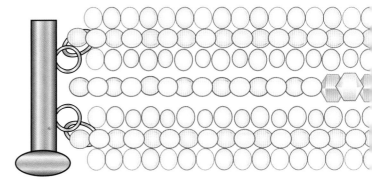

9 For all subsequent units, pick up 1D and pass through the next A in the strip. Pick up 1C and pass through the adjacent A from the other strip and the last C from the previous unit. Pass through the A from the first strip. Repeat this step until you have used the number of Cs determined by your calculation in step 3. At this point, substitute F for C until all 29 crystals are used, then switch back to C.

10 To finish, weave in your threads, tying a few half-hitch knots to secure. Trim the threads. To finish, insert a jump ring into the center of each corner unit and attach half of the clasp to either end of the bracelet.

Here you can see the reverse side of this lovely bracelet.

Crystal Twist

When I decided not to use LRAW ropes on my *Yo-Yo Reversible Pendant* (page 90), one of the reasons was that the strip wouldn't lie flat on the neck. After some analysis, I discovered the reason: the center bead on each face actually sits a little bit higher than the beads on the edges. I thought that maybe a twisted rope would look better, so I set about figuring out how to achieve a spiral with the same basic LRAW stitch.

I knew from my experience with twisted tubular herringbone stitch that a shift in the stitching path could cause a twist. So this time, instead of stitching the second layer in a parallel manner, I offset the attachment by one unit, which did in fact result in a twisted rope. One thing I like about this method is that the piece remains flat for most of the project, which makes it a lot easier to handle. It does make sizing a bit tricky, though, because it loses some length when the second half is stitched.

MATERIALS

3 grams 11/0 Permanent Finish silver seed beads (A)

60 purple velvet bicone crystals (B), 3mm

60 turquoise AB2X bicone crystals (C), 3mm

2 silver thread guards

2 silver jump rings

1 silver trailer-hitch clasp

SIZE

Makes a bracelet about 7½" (19cm) long

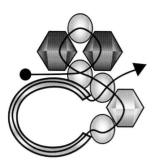

1 Use modified FRAW to create a double strip of beads for the base row. On a comfortable length of thread, string 4 beads in this order: ABAB. Pass through the first A. Pick up 1A, 1C, 1A and a thread guard. Pass through the first A of the second unit. Pass around the second unit again to secure the thread guard. This is row 1.

— TIP —

Keep a soft tension when stitching the base. The piece will tighten as you zip it up into the spiral.

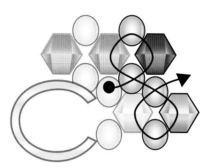

2 For row 2, pick up 1A, 1B and 1A. Pass through the adjacent B and the first A you picked up. Pick up 1A, 1C and 1A. Pass through the adjacent C and the first A you just picked up in the unit.

3 For subsequent rows, repeat the previous step until the strip is the desired length. One inch (3cm) of finished spiral needs about 8 base rows. On the last row, substitute a thread guard for the color B crystal.

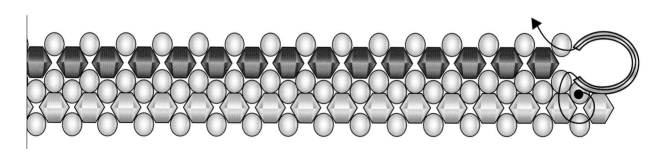

4 Continue through the next 3 beads of the last unit. Then continue through the A, thread guard and next A at the other end unit of the strip.

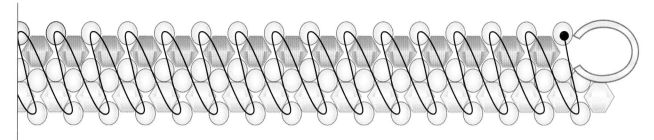

5 To zip up the piece, pass through the last outside A (adjacent to the C) on the opposite edge. Then pass back across the strip and pass through the second A on the first edge. Continue in this manner, passing through each subsequent A and pulling gently to work the strip into a spiral.

6 To finish, weave in your threads, tying a few half-hitch knots to secure. Trim the threads. Attach the clasp to the thread guards on each end with jump rings.

Detail of bracelet.

For a more casual look, use 8/0 seed beads and 4mm fire-polished beads.

Crystal Pathways

I really liked the way *Crystal Twist* (page 106) looked before the final step of twisting the base. So I decided to make a wider version. The resulting piece is soft and slinky, which is perfect for a night on the town—and it's still a superquick piece to stitch up.

MATERIALS

4 grams 11/0 Permanent Finish gold seed beads (A)

92 jet AB bicone crystals (B), 3mm

45 emerald AB bicone crystals (C), 3mm

1 gold 2-hole magnetic fold-over clasp

SIZE

Makes a bracelet about 7″ (18cm) long

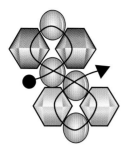

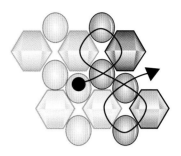

1 On a comfortable length of thread, string 4 beads in this order: ABAB. Pass through the first A to make a circle. Pick up 4 more beads in this order: ACAC. Pass through the first A to make a circle. This is row 1.

2 For row 2, pick up 1A, 1B and 1A. Pass through the adjacent B and the first A you picked up. Pick up 1A, 1C, and 1A. Pass through the adjacent C and the first A you just picked up.

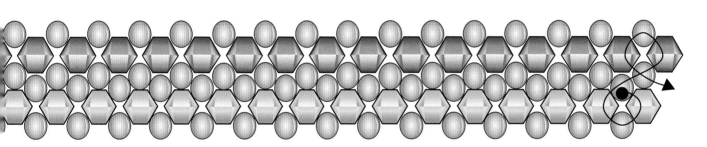

3 For all subsequent rows, repeat step 2 until the strip is the desired length. On the last row, complete the first unit only before moving on to the next step.

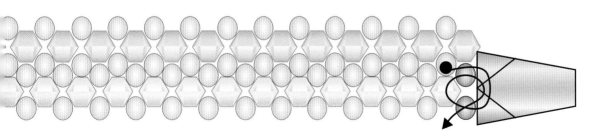

4 Pick up 1A and half of the clasp. Pass through the second hole of the clasp, pick up 1A, and pass through the last C and the first A you picked up in this step. Repeat the thread path several times to secure the clasp, ending with the thread coming out of the second A you picked up in this step.

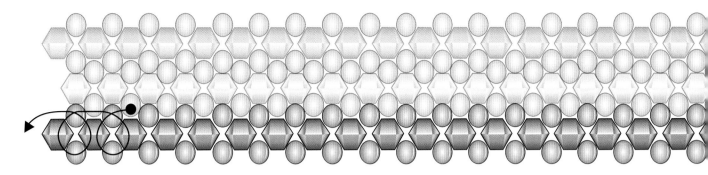

5 Pick up 4 beads in this order: ABAB. Pass through the first A to make a circle. Pass through the next A. Repeat down the length of the strip. Add one more unit of ABAB after passing through the last A in the existing row.

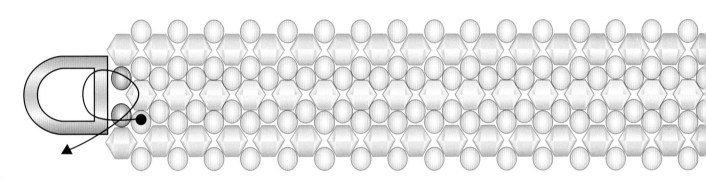

6 Pick up 1A and the second half of the clasp. Pass through the second hole of the clasp and pick up 1A. Pass through the last C in the strip and the first A you picked up. Repeat the thread path several times to secure the clasp. Weave in your threads and tie a few half-hitch knots to secure, then trim the threads.

Faux Ribbon Pendant

Soutache has become quite popular over the last few years, but as much as I like it, I have not found the time to learn the technique. One day I made a strip of LRAW, and I was folding and bending it when I noticed that it formed curves similar to those of soutache. I grabbed various sizes and shapes of accent beads and stitched them together into this sweet faux ribbon pendant. It hangs on a simple four-bead tubular herringbone rope.

— TIP —

This pendant is a great one for using up leftover bits and pieces from other projects. Choose a variety of pearls and crystals, arranging them however it suits you, to come up with a piece all your own.

MATERIALS

5 grams 11/0 Permanent Finish rose-gold seed beads (A)

5 grams 11/0 Permanent Finish silver seed beads (B)

16 maroon pearls, 2mm

92 matte green pearls, 2mm

1 8/0 Permanent Finish dark copper seed bead

2 green faceted fire-polished glass beads, 4mm

1 copper pearl, 6mm

2 chocolate brown pearls, 8mm

1 iridescent green pearl, 8mm

2 iridescent green coin pearls, 12mm

1 copper magnetic clasp, 6mm

SIZE

Makes a necklace about 19″ (48cm) long with a pendant about 2″ (5cm) wide and 1¼″ (3cm) tall

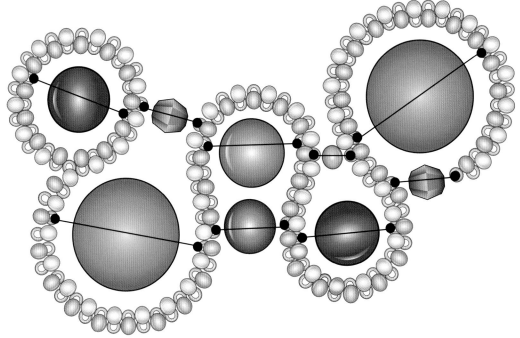

BEAD RIBBON

1 Create a 7" (18cm) strip of LRAW (see pages 96–97 for basic LRAW instructions, including the note in the sidebar). Use A (11/0) beads for the units in the base layer and B (11/0) beads for the placeholders. Then pick up only B beads to complete the second layer. My ribbon has 60 units in the base.

2 Attach the focal beads to the rope as shown in the diagram, using the center beads of the strip as anchor beads. Pass through each focal at least twice to secure. Maneuver through the strip along the edge beads to get to the next connection point. Attach the loose end of the rope as well.

BAILS

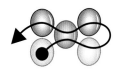

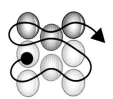

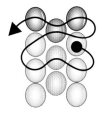

3 Stitch a 3-bead-wide peyote strip off the edge of the ribbon for the strap. To start, count out 11 A beads and 20 B beads. Weave through the work to exit a B along the top edge. Pick up 1A and pass through the next B in the edge. Pick up 1B and pass through the A you just added. Pick up 1B.

4 Pass through the first base B, the A added in the previous step, the second base B, and the first new B you added in the previous step. Pick up 1A and pass through the next up B. Pick up 1B and pass through the new A. Pick up 1B.

5 Pass through the B below the B your thread is exiting. Pass through the A and the next 2B. Pick up 1A and pass through the next up B. Pick up 1B and pass through the A you just added. Pick up 1B.

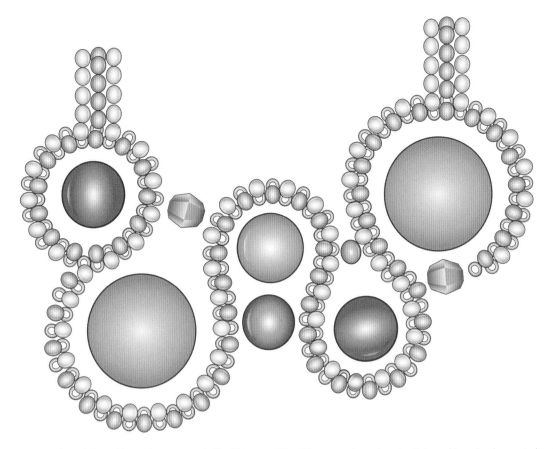

6 Repeat steps 4 and 5 until you have used all of the beads you counted out in step 3. Continue working in odd-count peyote stitch to connect the strap, using the existing beads on the other side of the ribbon instead of picking up new beads.

7 Repeat steps 3–6 for the second strap. Weave in your threads, tie a few half-hitch knots to secure them, then trim the threads.

8 The rope is a simple 4-bead herringbone tube (see page 12 for basic tubular herringbone instructions), with alternating A and B beads. After every 8 rows, add a 4-bead row with 2mm green pearls. Use maroon pearls for every sixth grouping. Attach the clasp to each end of the rope.

Circle Gets the Square

After designing several straight pieces with LRAW, I wanted to figure out how to make different shapes. A square was easy, as I just had to turn the row 90 degrees to make a corner. To make a circle, I started by using 3mm crystals as placeholders in the base row, which I knew would make the piece curve. After playing around with the bead counts and sizes, I succeeded in creating a sturdy circle. These shapes make great mismatched earrings, and finishing the back side of each piece assures they'll look great from any angle.

MATERIALS

1 gram 15/0 metallic wine seed beads (A)

2 grams 11/0 Permanent Finish steel seed beads (B)

3 grams 11/0 Permanent Finish galvanized wine seed beads (C)

13 purple velvet bicone crystals (D), 3mm

2 gunmetal thread guards

2 gunmetal ear wires

DIAMOND COMPONENT

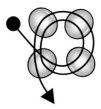

1 Use FRAW to create a diamond-shaped base layer with 7 units on each side. For the first unit, string 4B on a comfortable length of thread. Pass through the first B to make a square. Leave a 6" (15cm) tail. Pass through all 4 beads again, and pull snugly on the tail and working threads to tighten.

2 For units 2–7, pick up 1C and 3B. Pass through the adjacent B from the previous unit and the first B you picked up. Take care not to go through the C (the placeholder) more than once. Repeat 5 times. Continue through the next bead of the last unit.

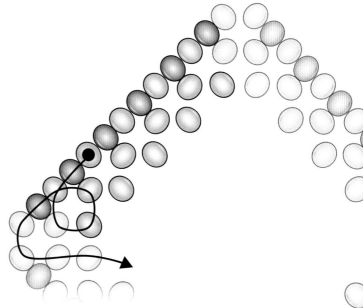

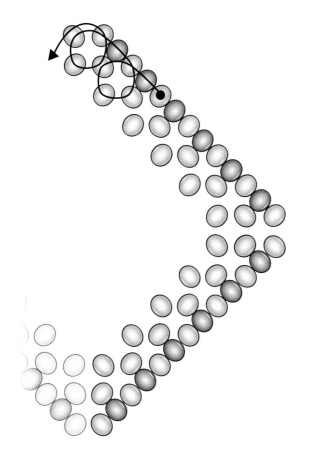

3 Repeat the previous step to add a second and third side to the diamond.

4 Pick up 1C and 3B. Pass through the adjacent B from the previous unit and the first B you picked up. Take care not to go through the C (the placeholder) more than once. Repeat 3 times. Pick up 1C and 1B. Pass through the B from the first unit as shown. Pick up 1B, pass through the adjacent B from the previous unit and the next B in the new unit. Pick up 1C and pass through the next 3B in the first unit and the next B in the following unit.

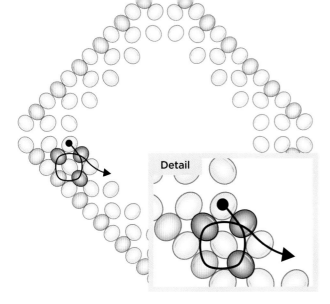

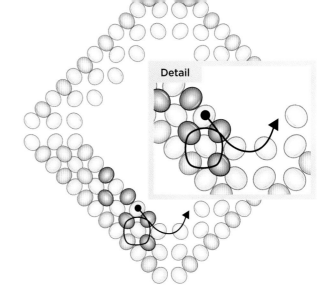

5 Create a layer of LRAW offset from the base layer. Pick up 2C. Pass through the opposite C on the other side of the strip. Pick up 1C. Pass through the first C you picked up in this step and the next B. This is unit 1.

6 For the subsequent units on side 1, pick up 2C and pass through the opposite C on the other side of the strip and the adjacent C from the previous unit. Pass through the first C you picked up and the next B. After the last unit is done, pass through the adjacent B to turn the corner.

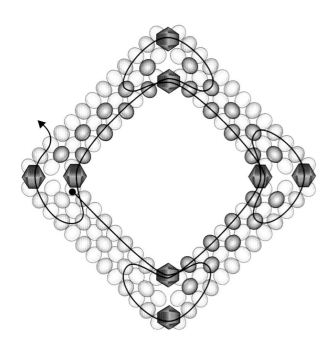

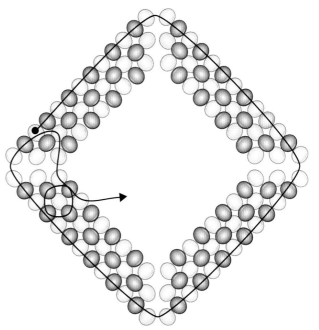

7 Repeat steps 5 and 6 all the way around the diamond, creating sides 2–4.

8 Pass through the edge beads to exit the last C on that side. Pick up 1D and pass through 3 beads of the next unit of the top layer. Pass through the next B and C. Pick up 1D and pass through the next 3 beads and next 2 beads in the unit on the top layer. Pass through the D and the inside edge beads to exit the end C on the next side. Repeat around the diamond, but on the last corner, after adding the last D, pass through the next B and move on to the next step.

9 To create a back layer, turn the piece over. Add 1C between each B along the outside edge of the diamond, mirroring the front of the work. Weave to the center. Add another layer of LRAW by repeating steps 5–7.

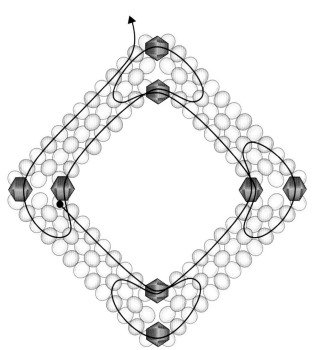

10 Repeat step 8 to add crystals to each corner. Continue along the outside edge to exit the last C.

11 Pick up 1B, 1C, 1B, a thread guard, 1B, 1C and 1B. Pass through the last C on the next edge. Weave through the work as shown to exit the last edge C on the first side. Repeat the entire thread path at least once to secure the thread guard.

12 Weave in your threads, tie a few half-hitch knots, and trim the thread. Attach the ear wire to the thread guard.

CIRCLE COMPONENT

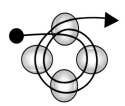

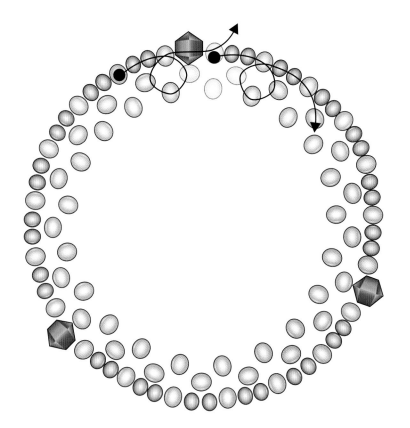

13 Use FRAW to create a round base. To start, string 4B on a comfortable length of thread. Pass through the first B to make a square. Leave a 6″ (15cm) tail. Pass through all 4 beads again and pull snugly on the tail and working threads to tighten. This is unit 1.

14 For units 2–20, pick up 2A and 3B. Pass through the adjacent B from the previous unit and the first B picked up. Take care not to go through the 2A (the placeholders) more than once. Repeat 18 times with the following placeholders: 2A 5 times, 1D, 2A 6 times, 1D, and 2A 5 times. Every seventh placeholder should have 1D instead of 2A.

15 For unit 21, pick up 2A and 1B and pass through the B from the first unit. Pick up 1B and pass through the next 2 beads of the new unit. Pick up 1D and pass through the next B in the first unit.

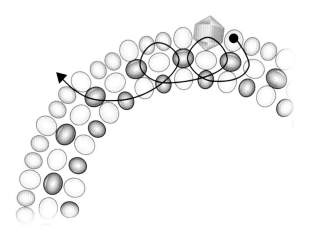

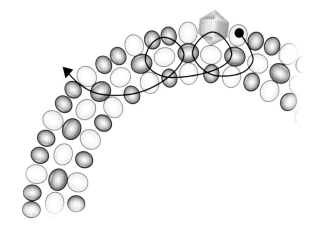

16 Pass through the next 2B in the unit. Pick up 1A and 1C. Pass through the last D added. Pick up 1C and pass through the A you just added and the next B in the strip.

17 Pick up 1A and 1C. Pass through the opposite 2A and through the last C added in the previous unit. Pass through the A you picked up in this step and through the next B in the strip. Repeat around the ring, substituting the D for the 2A as needed.

18 Flip the piece over. Weave to the outside edge and add 2A between each B in the ring, except for where there is already a C. In that case, pass through the C instead of adding new beads.

19 Repeat steps 16 and 17 to add another layer of LRAW to the back of the piece.

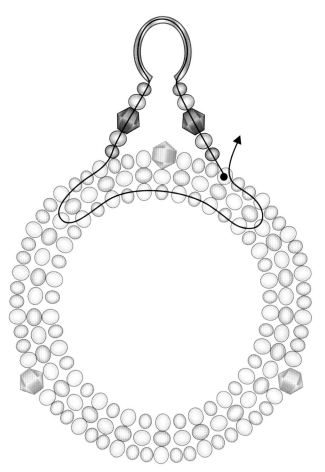

20 Pass through the work to exit the second B away from a crystal. Make sure you are headed toward the crystal. Pick up 1A, 1B, 1D, 1B, 1A, a thread guard, 1A, 1B, 1D, 1B and 1A. Pass down through the opposite B on the other side of the crystal. Pass through the work again to exit the original B. Repeat the thread path at least once to secure the thread guard.

21 Weave in your threads, tie a few half-hitch knots, and trim the threads. Attach the ear wire to the thread guard.

If you leave out embellishing the back side of your earrings, they will have a slightly more delicate look and feel, as shown in this color variation.

Kiss Me Quick

After making circles and squares, I wondered what other shapes I could make. I thought Xs and Os would be fun for a bracelet. Once I made the first X, I realized that a diamond shape would fit nicely between the Xs.

MATERIALS

6 grams 11/0 Duracoat seafoam seed beads (A)

6 grams 11/0 Duracoat eggplant seed beads (B)

52 turquoise AB2X bicone crystals (C), 3mm

SIZE

Makes a bracelet about 8″ (20cm) long

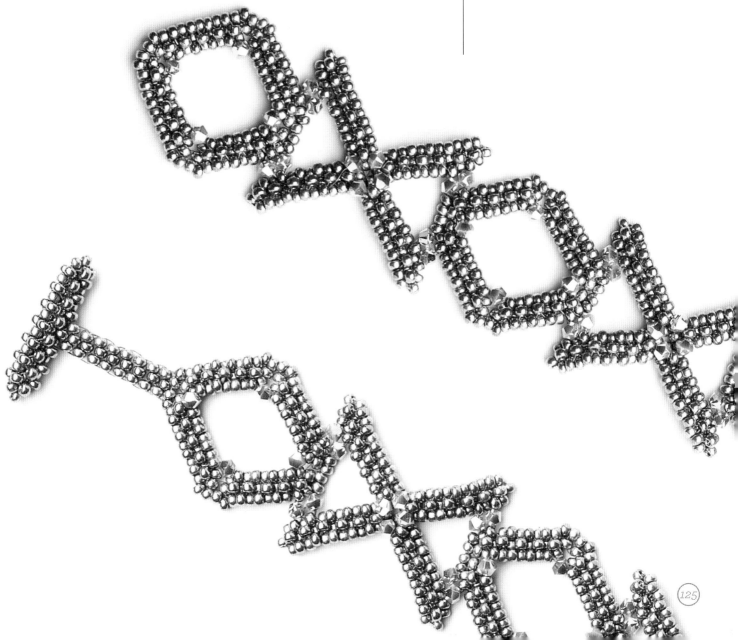

DIAMOND COMPONENTS

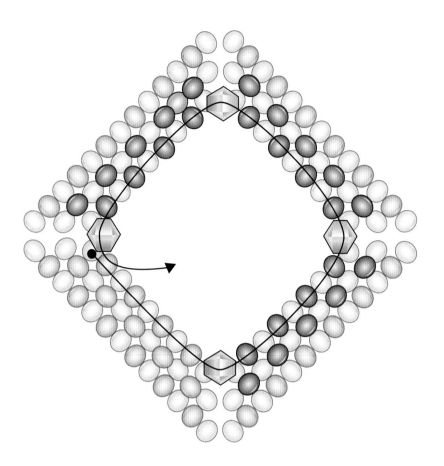

1 Repeat steps 1–7 of the instructions for the diamond component in *Circle Gets the Square* on pages 120–121, using A (11/0) beads for the base and B (11/0) beads for the placeholders and second layer beads (see pages 96–97 for basic LRAW instructions, including the note in the sidebar). Pass through the inner edge beads to exit the last B on that side. Pick up 1 C and pass through the end B on the next side. Repeat around. Set this unit aside.

X COMPONENTS

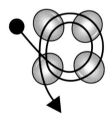

2 Use FRAW to create an X-shaped base layer with 7 units in each arm (the seventh unit in the center is shared). To start the center unit, string 4A on a comfortable length of thread. Pass through the first A to make a square. Leave a 6" (15cm) tail. Pass through all 4 beads again and pull snugly on the tail and working threads to tighten.

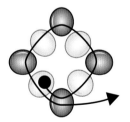

3 Pick up 1B. Pass through the next A in the previous round. Repeat 3 times. Pass through the first B. This is the center unit.

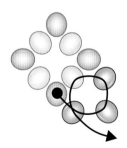

4 For unit 2, pick up 3A. Pass through the adjacent A from the previous unit and the first A you picked up.

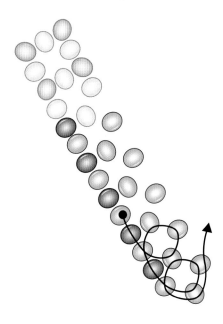

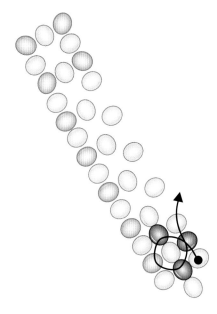

5 For units 3–7, pick up 1B and 3A. Pass through the adjacent A from the previous unit and the first A you picked up. Take care not to go through the B (the placeholder) more than once. Repeat 4 more times. Continue through the next 2 beads of the last unit.

6 Create a layer of LRAW offset from the base layer. For unit 1, pick up 2B. Pass through the opposite B on the first side of the strip. Pick up 1B. Pass through the first B you picked up in this step and the next A.

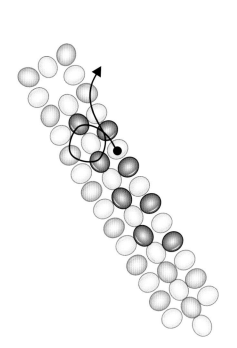

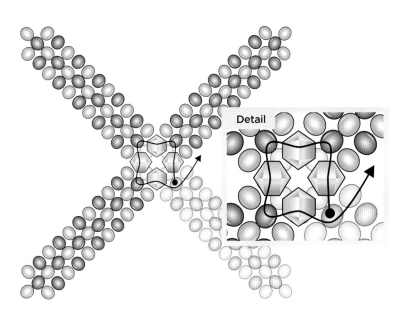

Detail

7 For units 2–5, pick up 2B and pass through the opposite B on the first side of the strip and the adjacent B from the previous unit. Pass through the first B you picked up and the next A. Repeat 3 times. After the last unit, pass through the next B in the center unit.

8 Repeat steps 4–7 to add 3 more arms to the component. Pass through the middle B on the first arm. Pick up 1C and pass through the next arm's center B. Repeat around the center. Pass through all 4 crystals several times to tighten the ring. Set this unit aside.

— TIP —

If thread shows between the central crystals, try picking up a 15/0 seed bead before and after each crystal to fill the space.

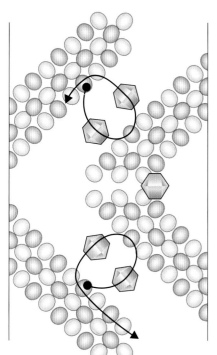

9 To connect individual components to each other, weave through the work to exit the second B from the end of 1 arm of an X component. Pick up 1C and pass through the second B from the end of 1 edge of a diamond component. Pick up 1C and pass through the B from the X component. Repeat the thread path at least once to secure the crystals. Repeat this step to attach all components.

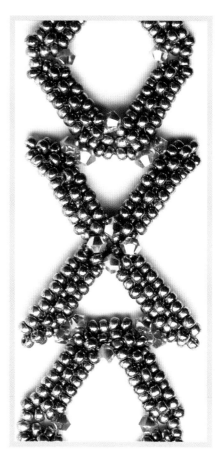

Detail of connections

— TIP —

The number of components you need for the bracelet may be fewer than you think. As the bracelet is worn, the diamond units will likely stretch horizontally, resulting in a more oval-shaped unit, which will take up more space.

10 To start the toggle bar, use a new thread to make a strip of LRAW with 8 units in the base. Use A color beads for the base and B color beads for the top layer.

— TIP —

Due to the elongating of the diamond units, my finished bracelet wound up much too large for me. So I threaded the toggle through the last diamond as well as the space between that diamond and the last X component for a better fit.

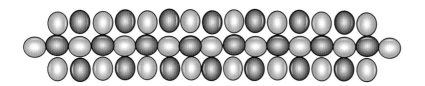

11 Add another layer of LRAW to the back of the strip with B beads. Place 1B between each A on 1 edge and work the back layer from these new beads.

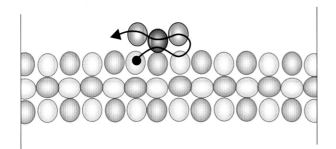

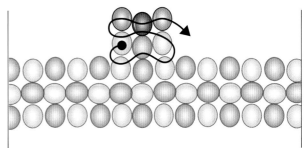

12 To attach the toggle bar, stitch a 3-bead-wide peyote strip off of the edge of the strip and attach it to the final component.

To do this, weave through the work to exit an A along the top edge. Pick up 1B and pass through the next A in the edge. Pick up 1A and pass through the B just added. Pick up 1A.

13 Pass through the first base A, the B you added in the previous step, the second base A, and the first new A you added in the previous step. Pick up 1B and pass through the next up A. Pick up 1A and pass through the new B. Pick up 1A.

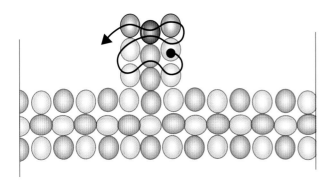

14 Pass through the A below the A your thread is exiting. Pass through the B and the next 2A. Pick up 1B and pass through the next up A. Pick up 1A and pass through the B you just added. Pick up 1A.

Option A

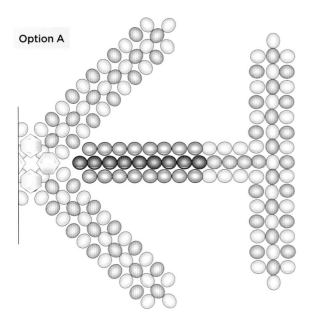

Option B

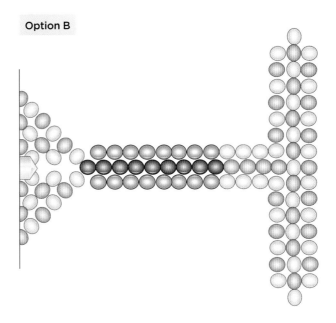

15 Repeat steps 13 and 14 until the strip is the desired length. The length of the toggle will depend on whether you have an X or a diamond at the starting end of your bracelet. If you start with an X, the strip will need to be longer. Attach the toggle to the final component by continuing the peyote. If your last unit is an X, refer to diagram Option A; if your last unit is a diamond, refer to Option B.

16 Weave in your threads, tie a few half-hitch knots to secure them, and trim the threads.

Cupola

After *Circle Gets the Square* (page 118) was made, I had to figure out if I could use the circle component as a bezel for a rivoli. This setting proved interesting, as the resulting piece did not lie flat but curved into a dome. I originally made a *Rosie Posie Rope* (page 48) to hang the pendant on, but it overpowered the piece too much. I went with something much simpler: a modified *Dainty Lace* (page 32) with a trailer-hitch clasp.

— TIP —

Substitute an 18mm Luna Cabochon for the rivoli for a different look.

MATERIALS

1 gram 15/0 metallic wine seed beads (A)

9 grams 11/0 Permanent Finish silver seed beads (B)

1 gram 11/0 Permanent Finish galvanized wine seed beads (C)

18 amethyst AB bicone crystals (D), 3mm

9 dark purple pearls (E), 3mm

12 maroon pearls (F), 4mm

9 maroon pearls (G), 6mm

1 volcano rivoli, 18mm

12 crystal magic red-brown SuperDuos, 2.5mm × 5mm

2 silver jump rings

1 silver trailer-hitch clasp

SIZE

Makes a necklace about 19½" (50cm) long with a focal piece 1½" (4cm) in diameter

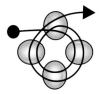

1 Use FRAW to create a round base layer. To start, string 4B on a comfortable length of thread. Pass through the first B to make a square. Leave a 10" (25cm) tail. This is unit 1.

— TIP —

Double-check your unit counts before connecting your circle. After step 2, you should have seventeen units with sixteen crystals. Add the last two crystals in step 3.

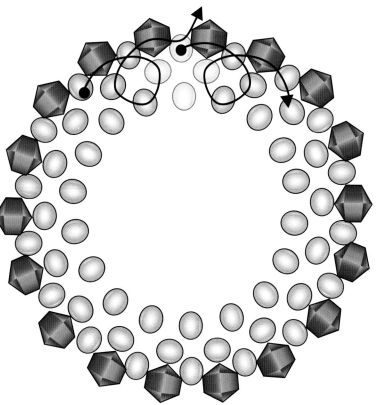

2 For units 2–17, pick up 1D and 3B. Pass through the adjacent B from the previous unit and the first B picked up. Take care not to go through the crystals (the placeholders) more than once. Repeat 15 times.

3 For unit 18, Pick up 1D and 1B and pass through the B from the first unit. Pick up 1B and pass through the B from the previous unit and the first B you picked up. Pick up 1D and pass through the next B in the first unit.

4 For unit 1 of the second layer, pass through the next 2B in the unit. Pick up 1A and 1C. Pass through the last D added. Pick up 1C and pass through the A you just added and the next B in the inside circle.

5 For units 2–17, pick up 1A and 1C. Pass through the opposite D and through the last C you added in the previous unit. Pass through the A you picked up in this step and through the next B in the inside circle. Repeat 15 times.

6 For unit 18, pick up 1A and pass through the adjacent C from the first unit. Pass through the opposite D, the C from the previous unit, and the A you just picked up.

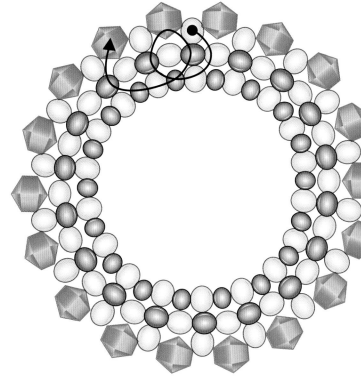

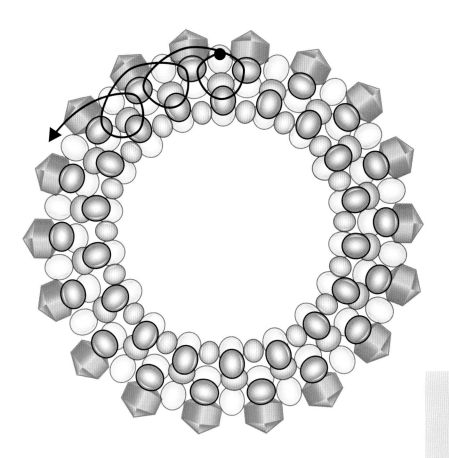

7 Flip the piece over. Weave to the outside edge, exiting a B. Pick up 3B and pass through the same B again and the next 2 beads in the edge (1D and 1B).

8 Pick up 2B. Pass through the adjacent B from the previous unit, the same B from the base round, and the next 2 beads in the base (1D and 1B). Repeat around the circle, but on the last unit, instead of picking up 2B, pass up through the adjacent B from the first unit and then pick up 1B. Pass through the adjacent B from the previous unit and the 3 base row beads.

— **TIP** —

Skip steps 7–9 to make a pendant without the rivoli in the center.

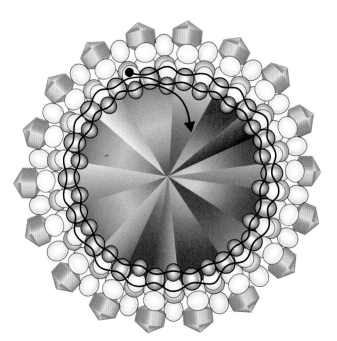

9 Pass through 2B to exit the center B in one of the 3 bead loops added in the last round. Insert the rivoli. Pick up 1B and pass through the next B in the round. Repeat all the way around. Step up to exit the first new B added. Pick up 1A and pass through the next B in the round. Repeat all the way around the circle.

10 Pass through the work to exit a B between an edge crystal. Pick up 7B. Skip the next 3 beads in the outer circle (D, B, D) and pass through the B. Keep the beads behind the crystals. Repeat all the way around. Step up by passing through the first 4 beads added.

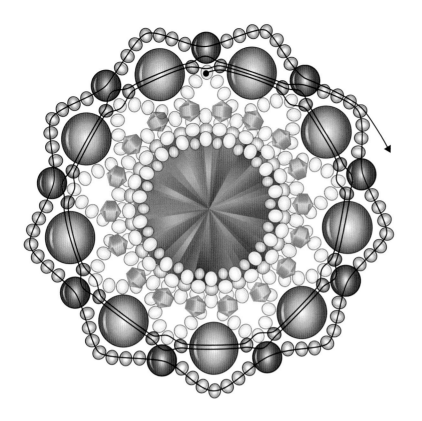

11 Pick up 1C, 1G and 1C. Pass through the center bead of the next 7-bead picot. Repeat around the circle.

12 Continue through the next few beads to exit a C just before the center B. Pick up 1E and pass through the next C. Pass through the 6mm pearl and the next C. Pick up 1E and pass through the next C. Repeat around the circle. End by exiting a 3mm pearl.

13 Pick up 7B and pass through the next 3mm pearl. Repeat around the circle. Pass through the first 4 beads added in this step.

STRAPS

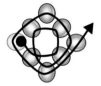

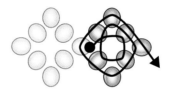

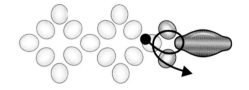

14 Use DDRAW to make the straps. For the first unit, pick up 4B. Pass through the first B. Pick up 1B and pass through the next B in the inner square just formed. Repeat twice more. Pass through the beads of this diamond to exit the B on the opposite side of the starting point of this step.

15 Repeat step 14 to add a second DDRAW unit.

16 Create an encircled SuperDuo (ESD) unit. To do this, pick up 1B, a SD and 1B. Pass through the corner B and the first B you picked up again.

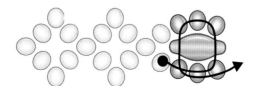

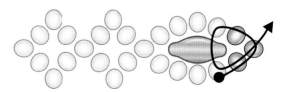

17 Pick up 3B. Pass through the second hole of the SD and pick up 3B. Pass through the first hole of the SD and the first 3 beads you picked up in this step.

18 Pick up 3B. Pass around the end of the SD and through the B on the other side. Pass through the second hole of the SD, the adjacent B and the next 2B.

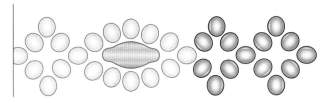

19 Repeat steps 14 and 15 to add 2 more DDRAW units.

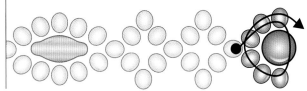

20 Make an encircled pearl (EP) unit. To start, pick up 3B, a 4mm pearl [1F], and 3B. Pass through the first 3 beads you picked up.

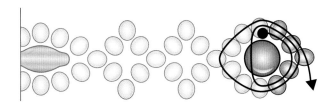

21 Pick up 4B. Pass through the B on the other side of the pearl, through the pearl, through the adjacent B, and through the first 2 beads you picked up in this step. Pick up 1B and pass through the second 2 beads you picked up in this step. Pass through the rest of the beads around the pearl, making sure that you pass through the corner B from the previous DDRAW unit. Exit the B on the end of the new EP unit.

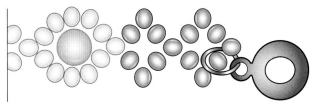

22 Add 2 DDRAW units, 1 ESD unit, 2 DDRAW units, and 1 EP unit. Repeat this pattern until the strap is the desired length. End with 2 DDRAW units. Weave in your working thread, tie a few half-hitch knots to secure, and trim the threads. Attach the clasp to the last DDRAW unit on each strap with jump rings.

— **TIP** —

The pearls in this strap are 4mm rather than 3mm as in Dainty Lace *(page 32). You may need to add another bead or two around each side of the pearl so that no thread shows.*

23 With your tail thread, weave through the work to exit the center bead of the net 2 pearls away from the first strap. Repeat steps 14–22 to add a second strap identical to the first.

Gallery

Shield of Itarildë

This piece was my entry for the 2013 International Battle of the Beadsmith competition.

Techniques: Circular herringbone variation, netting, right angle weave

Toblerone (Pearls and Pyramids)

Techniques: Modified cubic right angle weave, right angle weave, fringe

Principessa (Diamondback)

Technique: Tubular filled netting

Cosmos Necklace

Techniques: Right angle weave, tubular filled netting, netting, stringing

Fold Me Up

Techniques: Diagonal faux right angle weave, right angle weave

Pearl Cross

Technique: Cubic right angle weave

Claddagh

Technique: Right angle weave

Bella Tuscany

Technique: Right angle weave

Lunar Eclipse

Techniques:
Peyote, herringbone, twisted tubular herringbone, tubular filled netting

Quilt Cuff

This piece was featured on the cover of the Oct/Nov 2012 issue of *Beadwork* magazine.

Techniques: Right angle weave, cross weave

Index

Beadweaving Beyond the Basics. Copyright © 2015 by Kassie Shaw. Manufactured in China. All rights reserved. The patterns and drawings in this book are for the personal use of the reader. By permission of the author and publisher, they may be either hand-traced or photocopied to make single copies, but under no circumstances may they be resold or republished. It is permissible for the purchaser to create the designs contained herein and sell them at fairs, bazaars and craft shows. No other part of this book may be reproduced in any form or by any electronic or mechanical means including information storage and retrieval systems without permission in writing from the publisher, except by a reviewer who may quote brief passages in a review. Published by Fons & Porter Books, an imprint of F+W, a Content + eCommerce Company, 10151 Carver Road, Suite 200, Blue Ash, Ohio 45242. (800) 289-0963. First Edition.

a content + ecommerce company

www.fwcommunity.com

19 18 17 16 15   5 4 3 2 1

DISTRIBUTED IN CANADA BY FRASER DIRECT
100 Armstrong Avenue
Georgetown, ON, Canada L7G 5S4
Tel: (905) 877-4411

DISTRIBUTED IN THE U.K. AND EUROPE BY F&W MEDIA INTERNATIONAL
Brunel House, Newton Abbot, Devon, TQ12 4PU, England
Tel: (+44) 1626 323200, Fax: (+44) 1626 323319
E-mail: enquiries@fwmedia.com

DISTRIBUTED IN AUSTRALIA BY CAPRICORN LINK
P.O. Box 704, S. Windsor NSW, 2756 Australia
Tel: (02) 4560 1600, Fax: (02) 4577 5288
E-mail: books@capricornlink.com.au

SRN: T4095
ISBN-13: 978-1-4402-4268-7

Edited by **Noel Rivera and Christine Doyle**
Designed by **Ronson Slagle**
Production coordinated by **Jennifer Bass**
Photography by **Hannah Combs**
Author photo by **Jen Lepkowski**
Illustrations by **Kendra Lapolla**

Metric Conversion Chart

to convert	to	multiply by
Inches	Centimeters	2.54
Centimeters	Inches	0.4
Feet	Centimeters	30.5
Centimeters	Feet	0.03
Yards	Meters	0.9
Meters	Yards	1.1

About the Author

With her background in accounting, Kassie Shaw never expected to be a beadwork artist or a designer; but in 2006 she discovered beadweaving and since then she's be designing and creating off-loom designs. Her beaded bracelet, *Coronet*, was published in *Beadwork* magazine in December 2010. Since then, she has been published more than a half-dozen times and had a piece (*Quilt Cuff*) featured on the cover of *Beadwork* in 2012.

Kassie has taught at various bead shops and retreats. Her tutorials and kits can be purchased from her website at www.beadingbutterfly.com.

Try our other great beading titles!

Bead Metamorphosis
by Lisa Kan

Delight in a spectrum of sixteen beadweaving projects in *Bead Metamorphosis*. Create beautiful bead-woven earrings, necklaces, bracelets and brooches—all of which transform by disassembling, reassembling, reversing or interchanging separate beadwork components. Ideas and inspiration for multiple variations will lead to new metamorphoses, as you create stunning jewelry designs with multiple looks.

ISBN-13: 978-1-5966-8825-4

Mastering Peyote Stitch
Melinda Barta

Mastering Peyote Stitch provides a much-needed look into the integral peyote stitch technique. With fifteen styles in all, beaders will finally have an accessible, easy-to-understand guide to one of the fundamentals of beadweaving. Learn the basics of creating flat peyote bands, then advance to circular and tubular variations, eventually learning to fashion dimensional jewelry pieces. Once you've mastered the basics, dive into designing dimensional jewelry pieces and learn how to combine peyote with other popular bead-weaving techniques

ISBN-13: 978-1-5966-8633-5

Mastering Herringbone Stitch
Melinda Barta

Mastering Herringbone Stitch provides a solid overview to the second-most popular beadweaving technique—herringbone stitch. Learn the basics of creating flat bands, then advance into circular, tubular and spiral variations of the stitch. Additional chapters cover combining herringbone with other beadweaving techniques such as peyote stitch, square stitch, brick stitch, and right-angle weave. Twenty new step-by-step projects are included, with many variations.

ISBN-13: 978-1-5966-8632-8